"This book offers a creative lens for examining how to become a more responsive, innovative, and effective leader. It provides a unique and compelling perspective for improving your organizational efforts."

—**Don Finless**
President
The Onix Group of Companies, Ottawa, Canada
Design, animation, and IT solutions

"This book is a valuable resource for anybody who leads an enterprise in an increasingly complex, dynamic and global world. The AGILE approach delivers leadership and strategy that is effective and appropriate."

—**Eric Bohm**
CEO
World Wildlife Fund (WWF), Hong Kong

"*The Agile Business Leader* cuts straight to the core of today's challenge for business leaders driving a high velocity, global, and cross-generational workforce."

—**Paul Ringmacher**
Partner, Financial Services Technology
Capco

"In a current environment that often provides a dark backdrop for business, Barry and Eileen deliver a very timely message that precisely cracks the code for contemporary organizational success. *The Agile Business Leader* provides a formula of necessary leadership traits that will define success in the coming decade."

—**R. Karl Schlatzer**
Director, Global Business Development and Channels
SAS

"Historically, business leadership was autocratic and definitely 'top down'. What this book explores with fresh insight is how modern managers and leaders work with their teams to achieve results. AGILE leaders encourage original thought at all levels of the organisation and empower a far greater number of people."

—**Keith Butler-Wheelhouse**
CEO Smith's Group in London
Also served as CEO of Saab Automobiles in Sweden, chairman and CEO
of Delta Motor Corporation, and director, General Motors South Africa

THE AGILE BUSINESS LEADER SERIES

❖ The Agile Business Leader ❖

The Four Roles of Successful Leaders

No one leadership style is universally satisfactory. The leader who can listen, delegate, involve, decide, adapt, respond, and direct is the most successful over time. In an era filled with confusion, contradictions, and corruption, the world is calling for Agile Business Leaders.

❖ The Strategist ❖

ABL Theory in Practice

Strategists are always asking "What's next?" "Where else?" and "Why not?" They have an inquisitive nature, helping to create a sense of identity for people in their organization. Seeking large gains and unafraid to take smart, calculated risks, Strategists work on one simple rule: explore outside the boundaries with quantum-leap thinking.

❖ The Specialist ❖

ABL Theory in Practice

Specialists recognize that having a diverse knowledge and experience base enables them to assimilate novel ideas and connect seemingly discrete pieces of information. Specialists can quickly analyze a situation, make decisions, and act on opportunities.

❖ The Champion ❖

ABL Theory in Practice

Champions are responsive and authentic, regularly surpassing their personal goals by having the courage to do what is right. They grow excited about the possibilities that new ideas can bring. Champions personify corporate values and help form the character and strength of the organization.

❖ The Enabler ❖

ABL Theory in Practice

Enablers are not about authority; they are about influence, loyalty, and trust. They have strong collaboration skills and continually seek out ways to engage the masses and build organizations that continually learn, adapt, evolve, and improve.

THE AGILE BUSINESS LEADER®

THE FOUR ROLES OF SUCCESSFUL LEADERS

Eileen Dowse ❖ Barry Brewster

BROWSE PUBLISHING LIMITED

London ❖ *Hong Kong* ❖ *Sydney* ❖ *Dallas*

Email: info@agilebusinessleader.com

Website: www.agilebusinessleader.com

ISBN: 978-988-19468-1-2

Cover Design: Bonnie Brewster
Cover Composition: Craig Hines
Text Design: Craig Hines and David denBoer
Text Artwork: Gavin Coates
Cartaphors: GroupM, Firsttrack, Aedas
Typesetter: Craig Hines
Copyeditor: Maria L. denBoer
Proofreader: Bob Land
Indexer: Bob Land
Printed in Hong Kong

10   9   8   7   6   5   4   3   2

CONTENTS

THE ENABLER · 89

THE CHAMPION · 133

THE SPECIALIST · 159

CONCLUSION · 185

INDEX · 191

ABOUT THE AUTHORS · 200

ACKNOWLEDGMENTS

This book evolved over four years of working with thousands of people in their roles as leaders, employees, and learners. It is intended as a tribute to these people who shared their learning and frustrations with us over the years. *The Agile Business Leader* reflects the efforts and influences of many people. Certain people gave themselves to this work in large ways that call for special thanks.

We want to express our deepest appreciation to the unique leaders who were interviewed for this book, including Scott Andrews, Finn Boyer, Dan Duran, Patrick Carmichael, E'Vonne Cole, Jeff Daniels, Bobby Feilger, Leona Freed, Jeremy Gwee, Ian Hanna, Kay Holt, Howard Holtman, Mark Moran, Mark Patterson, David Roberts, David Spann, Karl Schlatzer, and Genelle Sharples. It has been a privilege to work with these individuals and gain clarity on their insights so we can share them with readers.

We also wish to thank the organizations, authors, and leaders who granted us permission to use figures, information, and quotes. We especially wish to acknowledge the leaders and staff at Evans & Peck for allowing us to use their case studies. It was here that our ideas were helped to incubate. We particularly thank GroupM, the Venetian Casino, Firsttrack, and Aedas, which agreed to share their Cartaphors with us and let others learn from their experiences.

We both want to especially thank our editors Maria L. denBoer, Veronica Miron, Ann Marie Nader, and Lyn Brewster, and our proofreader, Bob Land, whose sharp eyes, encouragement, and patience deserve a great deal of recognition. Their reviews provided thoughtful guidance and constructive feedback.

We thank our technical team, especially Ed Helvey who has been a fantastic support for us throughout this project. We are extremely grateful to our graphic designer Bonnie Brewster, who produced the book design concept, and Gavin Coates, who provided all the wonderful artwork throughout the book.

In addition, Eileen also thanks her wise friend Claudia Dubois, who helped to provide support and encouragement for completing this book. Eileen thanks her longtime friend Lauri Andrews, whose good humor and generous spirit endured many supportive phone calls and long talks as this book evolved. Finally Eileen knows that she could not have written this book without the faith and support of her husband of thirty years, David Dowse, and their children, Bryan, Kathleen and John.

Barry wishes to thank his "commercial mentor," friend and colleague Colin Jesse, who has guided his development in corporate governance and commercial reality over the past eight years. Without his support and guidance Barry would not have been a position to be able to write this book. Chris Brooks also provided patient and insightful support in helping to validate the concepts and models throughout the book.

Barry also thanks his inspirational and loving family, Lyn, Bonnie, and Martin Brewster, and mother Dorothy Barnes, who at 80-plus years is still an inspiration. As Tom Cruise said once, "You complete me!"

Note: We have made every effort to acknowledge the original creators of concepts presented in this book. If we have not succeeded in that endeavor we are sorry and would like to hear from you so that we can begin referencing your work.

INTRODUCTION

We began our collaboration in 2006 while sitting in a bar at a conference in Toronto, Canada. We had known each other for awhile and began sharing stories about the type of work each of us did. Not long after that discussion we decided to pool our diverse resources and experiences and produce this book—Eileen with her experience in building stronger working relationships and creating high-performing business cultures through executive coaching, facilitation, and leadership training, and Barry with his experience in facilitating change and strengthening business systems through organizational development and teaching clients how to adapt better to change and profit from emerging trends.

Our goal in merging our global experiences and insights was to develop a perspective of leadership that would help individuals and businesses increase productivity, efficiency, and profitability. Above all, we wanted to share our passion for helping leaders do a better job and positively impact the people they work with.

Since that time sitting in a bar and making notes on paper napkins, we sought out leaders from Asia, North America, Europe, and Australia and listened to their frustrations and successes. We noticed a groundswell of interest in creating productive organizations, given the depth and rate of change in the emerging global markets. The old mechanistic ways of leading and thinking no longer sufficed. Our clients needed to do something new. A wider variety of global competitors continued to flood the marketplace, the pressures to remain cost-competitive placed greater demands on organizations and their employees to work smarter and faster, and more and more they were being called on to take a more agile approach to leadership. They were being asked to be more resourceful, tactical, responsive, courageous, adaptive, accountable, collaborative, and customer focused, and to have the ability to provide a competitive advantage for the organization.

We know that today's business environment is more volatile. Organizations need to transform themselves regularly to stay ahead of shifting industry conditions and marketplace demands. The challenge for leaders in this new business environment is how to transform a reactive, constantly transforming organization into a strategic machine that creates ongoing business value.

During our conversations with leaders we kept hearing that in order for companies to be successful, they needed to leverage leaders' talents and work smarter, better, and faster. There is no doubt that the future will require new leadership attitudes and capabilities. Conventional wisdom would champion "structure and strategy" as the driving force of an organization, viewing businesses exclusively as rational enterprises. Our work and observations led to another conclusion. Our research for this book had shown that organizations were constantly calling for innovative leaders who inspire confidence and who can translate the corporate vision for their people and get the job done quickly. We found being an agile leader must now become conventional wisdom.

Leaders are beginning to understand the value of improved staff efficiencies, greater flexibility, faster time to market, and increasing focus on strategic flexibility. The demand has increased for leaders who can thrive in high-speed, rapidly changing, highly uncertain, and high-stress environments. Yet the quest for individuals to develop flexibility and responsiveness is still a tremendous need.

Logic, linear thinking, and rule-based analysis are no longer sufficient to succeed in the global economy. To survive in business today, leaders need big-picture thinking, flexibility in solving problems, and an innate ability to work well with people. The leader who can respond to environmental changes, lead and unleash innovation, improve project performance, and increase productivity is the one who will be the greatest asset to the organization. What organizations want is for their leaders to be agile.

This book is the first in a series of five books about the Agile Business Leader (ABL). This first book highlights the roles, traits, and competences of the ABL; the remaining four books go into more specifics.

WHY BECOME AN AGILE BUSINESS LEADER?

Why is leadership agility important to businesses? It comes down to the fact that everyone is seeing increased competition in their markets. Typically new players entering into the market do not arrive with the traditional structures and rules of older business models. These newer, often more vibrant innovative organizations move faster, get the first-mover advantage, and keep changing the rules, which stymies the more established organization.

Being agile has become a necessity, not a dream. Having the ability to adapt, change, and be responsive is needed in today's business environment. Organizations have to continue to re-architect, re-design, re-platform, and address globalization in order to move forward and work with their expanding customer base. This means organizations need to build flexibility into their operations and agility into their mindset in order to compete successfully. This also means organizations rely on leaders who can respond to these types of demands.

If you walk into any bookstore, the shelves are bulging with "how to," "when to," and "why to" books on leadership. There is no absence of leadership skills and theories being used in organizations these days. What we are finding as we work globally is an absence of *agile* business leadership skills being used. There are numerous leadership styles that have found their way into papers, articles, and books with each style having its own characteristics, strengths, and limitations, yet true leaders in today's economy must have the ability to view themselves from a third-person perspective and understand the role that is required of them. Agile leaders understand which "hat" they need to wear and are highly skilled in wearing it, allowing them to constantly keep pace with global nuances.

"According to 250 senior executives interviewed for 'An Agile Age,' a report by Gartner, commissioned by British Telecom, greater business agility will bring substantial savings and heavily influence the strategies and future spending priorities of UK public and private sector organizations. Those surveyed estimated that investments in making themselves more agile would result in a 4.8 per cent increase in workforce productivity equivalent to an addition of £20 billion to last year's GDP or a £4.3 billion contribution to profits. For the purpose of the study, Gartner defined the concept of 'business agility' as: 'The ability to demonstrate flexible, efficient and swift responses to changing circumstances by maximizing physical and human resources'" (retrieved February 18, 2010, from http://www.accountancyage.com/accountancyage/news/203 0365/agility-boost-uk-plc-profits-gartner).

Those interviewed in the Gartner study believed that increasing the ability to be agile needs to be a key organizational change initiative. They saw the ability to respond quickly to changing market circumstances as vital to future success. Becoming more agile was seen as the key to managing relationships and processes.

"By focusing on agile business processes, organizations are looking to become more flexible, cost-efficient, and customer-effective, all of which result in a direct impact on profitability. Meeting customer demands more efficiently and effectively has become a leading rationale for becoming more agile" (Gartner, April 6, 2007, How BPM Can Enhance the Eight Building Blocks of CRM, Marc Kerremans, Jim Davies).

It would seem that the Agile Business Leader would naturally begin to create an Agile Business Organization.

PURPOSE OF THIS BOOK

The purpose of this book, pure and simple, is to equip leaders to perform with excellence. It is designed to enable you to do your job better, faster, more accurately, and more efficiently and to be more economical—with less stress! *The Agile Business Leader* is designed to provide a common language for leaders at all levels. Our goal is to provide business leaders with a primer on practices and tools for functioning in a world of complexity, chaos, interdependency, and ambiguity. Developing leadership capabilities often requires changing people's mindset and altering their long-standing beliefs. It entails recognizing the causes and effects of peak learning and developing strategies for mental blocks, blind spots, and other barriers. This book offers readers some ideas that will withstand the test of time. An ABL thrives on communication and sharing of ideas and practices. This book is relevant to anyone who wants to begin understanding different insights and approaches for dealing with the human capital within her or his organization or team and accelerating results. It will identify aspects of building effective relationships, dialogue, and commitment. We know that good leaders develop through a never-ending process of self-study, education, training, and experience. This book requires that you be willing to learn strategies, recognize your own leadership style, and transfer knowledge to the workplace for improving collaboration, communication, and productivity. Regardless of whether you are a new or experienced leader, this book will help you to develop and strengthen your skills and enable you to take responsibility for your development. Although the concepts presented in this book were developed specifically for leaders, they are useful concepts for all individuals in all kinds of professions.

Information presented in this book can be used for

- Starting new initiatives.
- Maximizing the effectiveness of communications.
- Gaining a competitive edge.
- Exemplifying corporate governance.
- Mobilizing and incorporating existing talents.
- Creating paths to more profitability.
- Building collaborative cultures.

OVERVIEW OF STRUCTURE

In this book you will be introduced to concepts and tools designed to enable you to implement them into your own work. We have structured this book around the ABL model. Chapter 1 explains the elements of the model and the principles of being an Agile Business Leader. Chapters 2–5 elaborate on the four elements that constitute Agile Business Leadership, and Chapter 6 wraps up our thoughts about our methodology. These chapters will enable you to develop a broader understanding of the practical and theoretical aspects of leadership and give you the opportunity to learn more about a variety of perspectives on how to become more agile in your approach. At the end of each chapter we also have a section entitled "Questions to Consider." These questions are designed to increase your awareness of the ABL role and challenge some of your current thinking. They are designed to help you develop a more agile mindset. If you are leader with an interest in performance and productivity, we believe you will find great value in this book.

MESSAGE TO OUR READERS

We hope this book provides you with useful ideas and insights. We look forward to hearing about your models, approaches, and experiences as you read through this material. We are sure we have only begun to scratch the surface of developing Agile Business Leaders.

Please email us at mail@agilebusinessleader.com with your comments and ideas, or visit our website at www.agilebusinessleader.com.

1

THE AGILE
BUSINESS LEADER

How we do business is changing and how we need to lead during these changing times is changing even faster. The ability of leaders to play a role that is effective is the key to future organizational success. The developing Third World has no reason to behave by old rules and, in fact, has every reason to take extreme risks in pursuit of transcendent rewards. The old command-and-control models for leaders are being replaced by a new approach that fosters a highly collaborative, ethically based approach to achieving a positively focused "desired future state." With globalization and increased competition, organizations can no longer survive only on their past success, relying on the way they have always accomplished important matters. Leaders need to innovate, strive for the creation of new ideas and new products, and become more agile in their approach.

Founder and former CEO of Visa International, Dee Hock said in his book *Birth of the Chaordic Age*, "In the Chaordic Age, success will depend less on rote and more on reason; less on the authority of the few and more on the judgment of the many; less on compulsion and more on motivation; less on external control for people and more on internal discipline" (pp. 264–265). He defines "Chaordic" as the blending of chaos and organizing. He emphasizes the importance of developing principles that are not governed or explained by the rules but rather evolve and incorporate natural trends.

What Hock addresses is what we also believe—that is, it is not enough for an organization to simply respond, adapt, and cope with the pressures of change. Instead, organizations must create radically new uncharted ways to exceed customer expectations. This type of expanded thinking involves a more collaborative system and a new approach to leadership.

As the world of business changes so does the need for developing effective leaders who can respond to emerging issues. The question becomes, what is the most effective way to be a leader in this Chaordic Age which we are now living in?

LEADERSHIP

There are countless definitions of leadership. Perhaps the only common denominator is that a leader has willing followers. In essence, leadership is a process by which a person influences others to accomplish an objective and directs the organization in a way that makes it more cohesive and sound. Leaders help an organization build community by incorporating the followers' character, judgments, and efforts. It is the leader's role to build clarity of a shared purpose, formulate common principles, and develop the strengths of individuals. Leaders do this by applying their leadership capabilities, including their beliefs, values, ethics, character, knowledge, and skills. In this new world, leaders need to be adaptable, responsive, and resilient to changing conditions while at the same time preserving the overall cohesion and unity of the purpose for the organization.

Leaders in today's world must have a wide variety of capabilities. They must be able to initiate action to make things happen. Most important, they must be able to transform, adapt, and respond quickly. Today's leader needs to merge the reality of effectively impacting business capital with the more fundamental reality of developing the human capital of the organization.

A successful company can be defined on the basis of how well the leaders of the organization (1) leverage the skills and technologies used to create an advantage in the marketplace and build the business capital for the organization and (2) liberate human possibilities by having the capability to inspire, encourage, enable, and help people focus on operating at peak performance, therefore building the human capital for the organization.

We believe it is crucial to develop Agile Business Leaders to evolve companies so they can successfully navigate through the current changing global business environment.

Succession planning, including identifying key leaders and developing their leadership skills, is critical as businesses adapt. Leadership development in particular will be essential for an organization to sustain its competitive advantage as markets change. Good leaders develop through a never-ending process of self-study, education, training, and experience.

The ongoing issue every learning executive faces is aligning strategies with the needs of business. When a company brings together its highest-potential leaders in an intimate setting with the CEO and his or her team, an immediate benefit is gained. It is our intent that this book affects both your learning and your impact on the organization. We want to teach learning professionals how to realize and incorporate this immediate gain.

This book is used as a supplement to our Agile Business Leader program. During that program, we work with leadership groups over a period of one year, involving offsite meetings called "leadership summits" that last three days each. In between these leadership summits, group coaching occurs for improved learning and development.

AGILITY

Developing Agile Business Leadership is about shifting executive, middle management, and individual contributor mindsets away from hierarchical, bureaucratic, linear thinking systems and processes. It is about creating a positive momentum in leading organizations forward so they can respond quickly, be resilient to change, and build upon the shared knowledge of the organization. It is about developing an organization whose leaders are wise and innovative. Key determinants for an agile organization include leadership, culture, and values, along with an organizational process for adaptability and responsiveness.

In simple terms, traditionally there have been two "generations" of the organizational change process: Incremental Change and, in more recent years, Transformational Change.

1. *Incremental Change* follows a "quality assurance" approach to slowly and "incrementally" move an organization forward with minimal disruption. This is a relatively low-risk approach as it does not challenge existing assumptions or the organizational culture. It may also lead to the organization falling behind and stumbling. Each step within this type of system aims at an improvement in *degree*.

Incremental Change:
- Involves working within the current system.
- Is operational in nature.
- Relies on step-by-step improvements.
- Aims at changes by degree.
- Results in more of the same, only better.
- Is often implemented through a punitive system.
- Has low risk.

2. *Transformational Change* challenges an established framework and aims at renewal rather than refinement. Transformation is a change, not in degree (as in incremental change), but in *kind*. It is relatively high risk. It is fast and focuses on major conversion.

Transformational Change:
- Replaces established frameworks.
- Is strategic in nature.
- Creates a different way of thinking.

- Challenges assumptions.
- Knocks down walls for rebuilding.
- Is usually implemented through some form of "re-engineering" of the organization.
- Has higher risk than Incremental Change.

The Agile Business Leader gives birth to a new generation of change: Agile Change.

3. *Agile Change* leverages the knowledge and wisdom within an organization. It operates from a positive perspective within an organization. It focuses on the image of a desired future of organizational health and success to produce a change in energy levels and perspectives and a belief in a successful future.

Agile Change:
- Changes organizational psychology.
- Is personal in nature.
- Forms a new perspective on how to act.
- Changes behavior.
- Builds a sense of community.
- Creates energy and motivation to achieve.
- Requires leadership courage.
- Is implemented using collaboration and communication.
- Has low to moderate risk.

In our organizational development work with clients we promote the use of Agile Change because we have seen this approach produce sustainable, exponentially better, long-term, successful results.

Some of our clients who have used the Agile Change approach include:

– American Airlines, *the largest airline in the world*
– AS Watson, *the world's largest health and beauty retailer*
– GroupM, part of *WPP media conglomerate*
– Novozymes, *world leader in bio-innovations*
– Leighton Asia, *one of Asia's leading construction and mining contractors*

- Aedas, *the second-largest architectural firm in the world*
- United States Environmental Protection Agency, *a federal government agency, charged with protecting human health and with safeguarding the natural environment*

A tool we use with our clients to support change processes is the AGILE Strategic Planning Model. This model uses AGILE as an acronym and is based on the fundamentals of positive psychology to help individuals and organizations excel in their development and delivery. It is a method used to deliver sustainable and accountable work with increased commitment.

With the hectic pace of business, leaders and followers are being called on to be adaptive, flexible, and responsive to emerging trends and demanding customers. They are being asked to develop skills that ensure they provide value for the organization. These skills are seen as the key to staying ahead of shifting industry conditions and marketplace demands.

An Agile Business Leader thinks strategically and innovatively and is skilled in multitasking, involving

- Being able to leverage the knowledge and wisdom of everyone in the business.
- Being aware of her or his impact on people.
- Possessing industrial intelligence and the means to continuously gather more.
- Understanding the value of being customer-focused and strategically astute.

Taking an agile approach to development means a leader values the importance of human interaction and collaboration and knows that communication and sharing of ideas and practices is what makes organizations stronger and helps contribute to their success.

AGILE STRATEGIC PLANNING MODEL

Realism is the heart of execution. All strategic thinking approaches attempt to find an optimal match between the resources and capabilities available from the organization's strengths (and limitations) and the external market and environmental conditions, trends, opportunities, and threats. The matching between resources and capabilities results in a strategy that translates, hopefully, into performance. It is our experience that successful planning depends on widespread organizational involvement. It includes the involvement of resources, capabilities, key people, and stakeholders in the preparation to identify critical issues and make emerging needs easier to identify. For this reason, we created the AGILE Strategic Planning Model. We wanted a tool to give our clients to assist them with

- Expanding their thinking.
- Building on their strengths.
- Enlisting support for action.
- Implementing a plan.

The AGILE model is based on the fundamentals of positive psychology. It is a method used to create a positive "can do" attitude to the future and therefore empower individuals and organizations to excel in their growth and deliver sustainable, accountable, and excellent work. When a leader takes a *non*-positive approach, or what is commonly known as a deficit or gap-based approach, to strategic thinking, the organizational issues become problems to be solved. Action plans are created to rectify the problems and gaps in performance.

When a leader uses a positive approach to strategic thinking, the organization's entire system becomes a solution to be incorporated into the plan for moving forward. The answers in strategic thinking lie within the talent, wisdom, and drive of the employees. With the AGILE model, strategic dialogue occurs within the organization, which we have experienced as essential for strategic thinking to take place.

When a leader is truly an Agile Business Leader, the preferred approaches to strategic development mean value is placed on the importance of human interaction and collaboration. An agile thinker knows that communication and sharing of ideas and practices are what make organizations stronger and help contribute to total and sustainable success. This kind of positive approach to strategic thinking allows people to be open about the current situation and focus positively on creating their collective desired future state. It creates alignment and a unified commitment toward a common mission. This AGILE Strategic Planning Model focuses on reaching the desired future state by empowering people to create strategies for success in leveraging their existing strengths.

Below is a diagram to further explain this model.

The following are the steps to take in this progressive model. We have also included the purpose for each step, a question to ask to begin getting into the right mindset, and a question that must be answered "yes" to ensure you have made the most of your thinking and innovative talents.

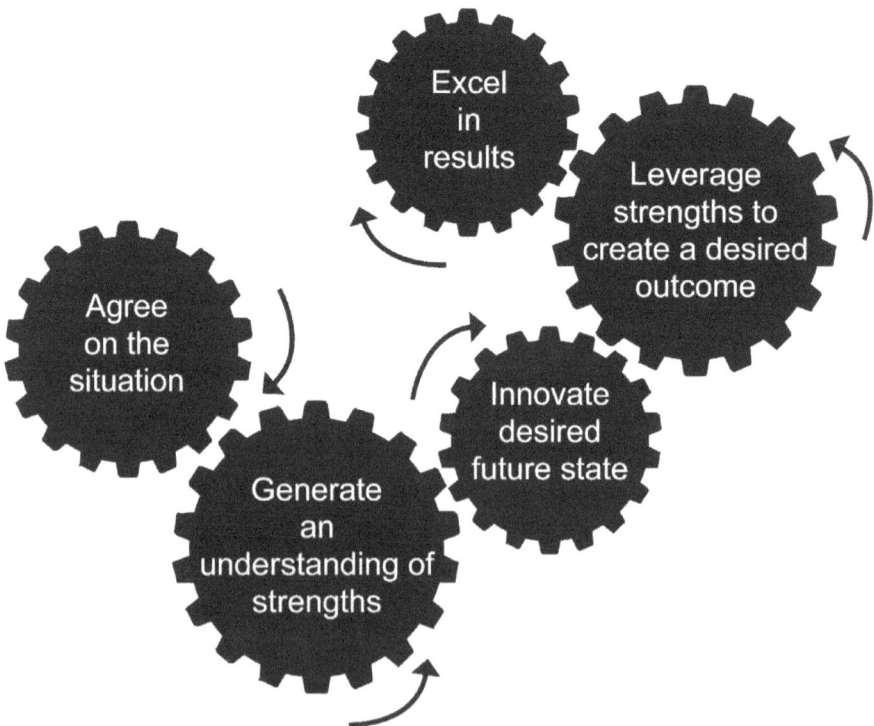

A G I L E Strategic Planning Model

A—Agree on the Situation

Purpose of this step: Recognize and understand the situation facing the individual, team, or organization and help ensure alignment on the situation.

A question to prompt thinking: Based on your understanding, what situation is currently affecting performance?

Process step confirmation: Does everyone who needs to be involved understand the situation?

❐ Yes   ❐ No

G—Generate an Understanding of Core Strengths

Purpose of this step: Recognize specific strengths and capabilities that are accessible for use.

A question to prompt thinking: What strengths are available within the network? *Note:* Strengths can include procedures, systems, finances, competencies, partnerships, resources, individuals, attitudes, culture, and behavior.

Process step confirmation: Are we clear on our available strengths?

❐ Yes   ❐ No

I—Innovate the Desired Future State

Purpose of this step: Create clarity and alignment on what is seen as the optimal future state.

A question to prompt thinking: What outrageous possibilities could occur in eight years or more to have an enormous impact on this situation?

Process step confirmation: Have we gone beyond the realm of possibilities for what could be achieved?

❐ Yes   ❐ No

L—Leverage Strengths and Create Desired Future State

Purpose of this step: Ensure the strategies or initiatives are aimed at achieving the desired future state and leverage available strengths.

A question to prompt thinking: What strategies are needed for creating the future we want?

Process step confirmation: Have we searched and incorporated high-leverage points (strengths) in our strategies to make a difference?

❒ Yes   ❒ No

E—Excel in Results

Purpose of this step: Create plans, assign roles and responsibilities, and develop actions for success.

A question to prompt thinking: What are the roles, responsibilities, and actions needed to implement each initiative or strategy?

Process step confirmation: Have we developed clarity around the committed plan?

❒ Yes   ❒ No

We can't clone people, but we can adopt their successful behaviors and strategies for nurturing innovative and breakthrough thinking. Our experience shows us that organizations do not get on board and implement plans unless the right people, individually and collectively, focus on the right details at the right time and are supported by the right conditions. The AGILE Strategic Planning Model is designed as a process for generating powerful ideas and for energizing people to believe the process is worthwhile and will occur at the right time.

By using the AGILE Strategic Planning Model, a leader can energize people and enhance strategic outcomes by

- Developing faster organizational processes and increased productivity.
- Building global organizational capabilities by developing the next generation.
- Building values and principles for effective leadership.
- Increasing shareholder value.
- Attracting, developing, and retaining talent.
- Improving open communication for free and beneficial exchanging of ideas, solutions, and discoveries.

The A G I L E Model puts the spotlight on strengthening what is already working. It develops openness among people. It creates energy and enthusiasm by developing an atmosphere for generating agile strategic solutions. This approach becomes a joint venture from which everybody learns. Creating an "agile enterprise" using Agile Strategic Thinking promotes a positive culture, which is critical when working in an ever-changing global economy.

AGILE BUSINESS LEADER (ABL)

From our experience in working with organizations from around the world, the major component of fundamental success for any business is ensuring the development of leaders—more specifically, developing Agile Business Leaders who help transform the business and make it thrive in the face of adversity. It is Agile Business Leaders who work with both the business and human capital components and are adaptive in their approach. They are not focused only on doing things one way. They provide instant feedback for personal and business development and strive to continuously improve. ABLs value the importance of human interaction and collaboration and know that communication and the sharing of ideas and practices is what makes organizations stronger and more responsive to customer needs.

ABLs are comfortable dealing with widespread ambiguity and never-ending change. We say, "They can roll with the changes." The best organizations, whether they know it or not, develop Agile Business Leaders who leverage the knowledge and wisdom of the organization through their roles as Enabler, Champion, Specialist, and Strategist as the situation requires. Playing all these roles becomes necessary for leaders in today's frantic world.

ABLs are Enablers. They enable people to act and inspire outstanding performance. They are resilient to breaks in communication channels because they have strong collaboration skills and continually search for ways of engaging the masses and building organizations that continually learn, adapt, evolve, and improve. They do not get stuck on the petty details or emotional dramas that can distract the focus from where it belongs. Rather, they have the innate ability to impart a sense of invincibility, power, and control over the situation. They are incredibly driven, which rubs off on their followers. They tap into reserves of the minds, hearts, and souls of people and know which buttons to push to activate their staff's faith, hope, drive, and perseverance. Enablers are not about authority; they are about influence, loyalty, and trust. They communicate an optimistic, bright, enticing picture of the future for their followers. They convince people to get on board and stay on board. They make people feel good about themselves, and they make others feel good about what they're accomplishing.

ABLs are Strategists. They expect that things may not go as planned, and they thrive on unplanned opportunities. They create the future by visualizing it and collaboratively building a plan for success. They are intuitive, and their vision is based on ethical business values. They are always asking "What's next?" "Where else?" and "Why not?" Because of this inquisitive nature, they help create a sense of identity for those in their organization. They galvanize followers by keeping interest and motivation high. They recognize that interest and motivation are never at the peak at all times even in the best of teams and places. No matter where people are and what they are doing, sooner or later there is work that is neither particularly interesting nor motivating and they have to slog through it to get the work done. If people are motivated and interested in their project they will see that what the leader is doing is part of the big picture, or they simply trust that it is with the right intent and get through it. ABLs are big thinkers, and their actions are large and daring. They seek large gains and are not afraid to take smart, calculated risks. ABLs work on one simple rule: explore outside the boundaries. Quantum-leap thinking is a regular exercise for ABLs. They convince followers to discard their policy and procedures manuals and instead create commonsense, flexible, and ethical guidelines. They design their organization's infrastructure to support every aspect of innovation by helping to create or modify the organization's collective values, beliefs, attitudes, and behaviors.

ABLs are Specialists. They not only gain knowledge, expertise, and wisdom, they also use the collective intelligence of those around them to build an understanding on how to be as effective as possible. Specialists know that having a highly diverse and broad base of knowledge and experiences will enable them to assimilate novel ideas and connect seemingly unconnected pieces of information. To this end, they aggressively hunt and gather ideas and opportunities before others are even aware of the need to do so. They strive to continually grow their knowledge base and convert it into value for the target market. They study trends and technological developments and are focused consumers of knowledge and information. They are continuous sponges for information and experiences and incorporate all they have learned to be specialists in their field. Leaders using this role are quickly able to analyze a situation, make decisions, and act on opportunities. In their quest for improving the status quo, they search out ways to form shortcuts to slash red tape.

ABLs are Champions. They recognize that speed and responsiveness have become even more important for business survival. Getting people excited about performing quality work, staying committed to the cause, and moving forward toward profitability are major components for overall success. Champions are responsive, authentic, and willing to expose themselves by having the courage to do what is right. They get excited about the possibilities new ideas can bring. Champions personify corporate values and help form the character and the strength of the organization. They have the courage to stand up for what they believe and have a strong orientation toward achievement. They have high expectations for themselves and for others and always push to achieve. In short, the Champion's role is about the leader's character.

HOW IS AN ABL DIFFERENT FROM OTHER TYPES OF LEADERS?

Traditional leadership styles typically fall in one of three categories: autocratic, democratic, or laissez-faire. Autocratic leaders dominate team members, using a unilateral approach to achieve a singular objective.

This approach to leadership generally results in passive resistance from team members and requires continual pressure and direction from the leader in order to get things done. Democratic leaders make decisions by consulting with their team, while still maintaining control of the group. Democratic leaders allow the team to decide how the task will be tackled and who will perform which task. Laissez-faire leaders exercise little direct control over their group, setting general direction and then leaving the team to sort out their roles and tackle their work, without the leader participating in details. These styles are based on theories that hinge on the belief that power and control are bestowed on leaders because of their position. These leadership styles work on the premise that leaders are followed because of personal loyalty to the position (he's a VP, she's the CEO) rather than to the personal traits of the leader. No matter how you categorize leadership styles or whether you use a competency, behavior, contingency, or transformational perspective to define leadership, the basic assumption is that leaders "make a difference." They align people and organizational goals to achieve results.

For Agile Business Leaders, the main focus goes beyond position and power. ABLs emphasize the link between business capital and human capital. ABLs incorporate the ingenuity, resourcefulness, skills, and abilities of each team member and leverage the resources of the organization in building opportunities and solutions. Whereas a traditional leader would direct a team using his or her authority, an ABL involves all stakeholders, incorporates the business vision, and collaborates to get the work done.

The fundamental difference between traditional and agile leadership is found in the way change is handled. Traditional leadership looks to eliminate and stabilize change by completing a list of actions and formulating new systems and strategies. Agile Business Leaders accept that change is an everyday occurrence and an opportunity for growth. ABLs ferret out gateways for change and leverage the strengths of individuals and groups to create reliable and efficient solutions. They help to create a sense of ownership in the task.

Over the years, we've seen leaders with command-and-control mindsets doom entire organizations to mediocrity or sheer survival. We promote the development of the Agile Business Leader mindset, one that is grounded in a radical shift in perspective about how organizations operate when leaders positively leverage their capabilities, and exhibit the courage to adapt and face the challenges of the new strategic reality with agility.

ABL PRINCIPLES

ABL Principles are proven guidelines to enhance effectiveness. These eight principles serve as the underlying criteria for operating successfully in today's global business environment. In short these principles are about having the capacity and willingness to apply *commitment*, *wisdom*, and *innovation* to everything you do.

1. Attitude Determines Results

   A problem can either be an obstacle or a challenge, depending on your attitude. When Henry Ford, founder of the Ford Motor Company, said, "Whether you think you can or you think you can't, you are right," he was expressing this principle. It is valuable to remember that your attitude greatly affects your experiences, expectations, beliefs, and level of success. For the agile thinker, obstacles and issues are seen as an opportunity and simply a way to look at things from a different angle.

   "Attitude Determines Results" is about being adaptable, flexible, energizing, and willing to adjust to change. For this principle, use the power of the question, *"Why not?"*

2. There Are No Limits

   Every problem has more than one solution; therefore, do not be held back by an apparent lack of possibilities. Leaders often block their potential achievements by thinking they can't do something or they don't have the resources or support to achieve what they want. These leaders block their own success. They often get stuck in one method, one process, one technique, or one goal, and if it does not work they simply shout louder or give up. ABLs know that creativity and innovation are only limited by the range of a person's perceptions and have the flexibility to realize there is always another way to do something. They reach high and wide for solutions.

"There Are No Limits" is about being courageous, resourceful, resilient, quick, and responsive. For this principle, use the power of the question, *"What if?"*

3. Power Comes from Within

Whether you choose to use it or not, you have power. Peak Performance guru Anthony Robbins states in his book *Unlimited Power*, "The ultimate power is the ability to produce the results you desire most and create value for others in the process" ([New York: Fawcett, 1986], p. 5). Power is often based on expertise, ability, position, and access to information. Real power lies within the person who can enhance the achievement of the group, the quality of relationships, and a group's adaptation to the environment, at the same time making the responsibility of any action shared rather than imposed. For the agile thinker, real power requires self-awareness and the ability to engage people toward desired results.

"Power Comes from Within" is about being engaging, active, focused, encouraging, and productive. For this principle, use the power of the question, *"How does my leadership impact people?"*

4. Positive Positioning Affects Direction

The business world is extremely diverse, with continually evolving challenges. This principle speaks to viewing and managing a situation as a positive opportunity. In an interview with a Hong Kong newspaper in May 2007, Edward de Bono was quoted saying, "Studies show that 90% of error in thinking is due to error in perception" (retrieved from "All in the Mind," an article in the Hong Kong *South China Morning Post*, May 27, 2007). Perceiving issues as opportunities propels people toward clear, quick, and effective solutions. Taking a more positive approach to "issue resolution" is exponentially more effective than "fixing weaknesses." Possibilities and positive thinking support the ABL's efforts, and they will use the best means at hand to keep results coming.

"Positive Positioning Affects Direction" is about being positive, being ready to accept change strategically, and being able to leverage strengths and opportunities. For this principle, use the power of the question, *"How can we leverage what exists to create something better?"*

5. Knowledge + Action = Results

Knowledge is only useful if you act on what you know. Author Gersham Bulkeley wrote, "Actions are more significant than words," (*Will and Doom, or The Miseries of Connecticut by and under an Usurped and Arbitrary Power* [Philadelphia, 1692]), and he was right. Regardless of the industry, knowing what to do is not enough. Organizations succeed in a global economy because they turn knowledge into action. The agile thinker is someone who knows how to gather and process sector and organizational intelligence. Agile thinkers dare to get involved, to act, to execute, and to implement. They are successful because they can lead in the delivery and completion of a project.

"Knowledge + Action = Results" is about being up-to-date on industry trends, customer-focused, and a lifelong learner. It is about having the ability to act intelligently and courageously. For this principle, use the power of the question, *"Where can I improve in my knowledge and in my actions?"*

6. Character Makes a Great Leader

Character is built by thought, choice, courage, and determination. Choosing the right way might not always be the easiest way. Having the courage to stand up for what is right and raise issues/ objections, especially when it is inconvenient or unpopular to do so, is a true test of moral character. Rules cannot substitute for character. Leaders' moral purpose is simply part of their character. The American actor Paul Newman said, "A man with no enemies is a man with no character" (*Paul Newman: A Life in Pictures*, ed.

Yann-Brice Dherbier and Pierre-Henri Verlhac [2006], p. 120).
Character is the indelible mark that determines the true value of
all your work. Experiences, trials, and sufferings build a person's
character. To have a good character is to have honesty, integrity,
spontaneity, and empathy.

"Character Makes a Great Leader" is about being accountable,
loyal, and honest and acting with integrity in unpredictable situations. For this principle, use the power of the question, *What do I
stand for and whom do I represent in that thinking and in my
actions?"*

7. We Are All Global Citizens

We are all citizens of the planet earth. Global citizenship is about
living responsibly, regarding all human beings as fellow citizens, and
being proactive in seeking the common good. It is about universal
fairness, reducing total environmental impact, and caring for human beings and the world/planet in its entirety. Global citizens are
responsible to society by being an economic, intellectual, and social asset to each country and community in which they operate
in. Agile Business Leaders are aware of their business and industry
sector within this global context. They are also aware of how the
globe impacts them. Global citizens are all those who work to
make the world a better place and include activists, businesspeo-
ple, reformers, politically conscious nationalists, and leaders.

"We Are All Global Citizens" is about being collaborative and
creating productive relationships that are inclusive and customer
focused. It is about individuals living, working, and playing within
the transnational norms and status that defies national boundaries and sovereignty. For this principle, use the power of the question. *"Am I doing the right thing or just doing things right?"*

8. Authenticity Defines Character

Authenticity is not only a state of awareness, it is a state of being.
The authentic person is centrally concerned with ethics and moral-
ity and with deciding what is significant, what is right, and what
is worthwhile. Being authentic is being genuine and true to com-

mitments and living with unquestionable congruence. It is the alignment of sincere thoughts, values, emotions, and actions and not a means of hiding behind a mask, faking thoughts or feelings, or using a spin to promote a sanitized version of the truth. The psychologist Abraham Maslow said, "You learn to be authentic, to be honest in the sense of allowing your behavior and your speech to be the true and spontaneous expression of your inner feelings. Authenticity is the reduction of phoniness toward the zero point" (*The Farther Reaches of Human Nature* [New York, 1971], p. 183). Authentic leaders know they are neither a copy of no one nor a counterfeit of the real thing.

"Authenticity Defines Character" is about being authentic to and with yourself, rather than living vicariously off the visions, understandings, values, and beliefs of others. Being authentic is living with honesty and integrity where nothing is false, imitative, or imaginary. For this principle use the power of the question, *"Are my words and actions congruent with my beliefs and values?"*

ABL ASSESSMENT

How do you know if you are an Agile Business Leader? Agile Business Leadership is more than a mindset; it is a set of roles, traits, and competencies. It incorporates talent management that is generally driven by competency profiles, higher-level information, the identification of required skills, and specific knowledge, proficiency levels, and behavioral descriptions.

Before we give a more in-depth explanation of our theory and the ABL model, we thought you might be interested in taking a quick assessment to determine your strengths as an ABL. This assessment incorporates the four roles involved in being an ABL: (1) Specialist, (2) Strategist, (3) Enabler, and (4) Champion. Within these roles are sets of traits and competencies that leaders must possess or develop for responding quickly, being resilient to change, incorporating knowledge learned, and developing an organization whose leaders are wise and innovative.

The following list of traits and their competencies sets a high standard for anyone currently serving in a leadership role or aspiring to be an

ABL. Some of our clients have incorporated this assessment into their performance review process, and others have used this assessment as the beginning to valuable conversations for improving business operations. As part of our ABL program we also include an in-depth online personality assessment to increase awareness of ABL behavioral patterns.

(Text continues on page 30.)

Specialist	Possesses knowledge and professional competence relative to work function.			
Behaviors Please rate yourself in the following criteria areas	1 = low 4 = high			
Stays current in terms of professional development.	1	2	3	4
Knows when and where to obtain assistance when faced with challenging work problems.	1	2	3	4
Applies expertise to perform the job effectively.	1	2	3	4
Refers individuals to available resources to help further their success.	1	2	3	4
Continually seeks sources of information or subject matter experts to maintain current knowledge.	1	2	3	4
Analyzes pertinent information to better understand its impact prior to making decisions.	1	2	3	4
Holds people accountable by delegating power and responsibility.	1	2	3	4
Learns, develops, and demonstrates technical and functional expertise in area of responsibility.	1	2	3	4
Uses facts, input from systems, input from others, and sound judgment to reach conclusions.	1	2	3	4
Total for Specialist Add the numbers you circled in each column and record the sum in the box for that column.				
Add the scores in the four boxes for your Specialist competency score.				

Strategist	Recognizes and acts in a timely and decisive manner as rapid changes occur in the global economy.			
Behaviors *Please rate yourself in the following criteria areas*	1 = low 4 = high			
Clearly communicates the vision/goals of the organization, helping others to understand their role and expectations for achieving the business plan.	1	2	3	4
Builds commitment, pride, organizational spirit, and strong relations for enhancing group efforts.	1	2	3	4
Installs changes for pursing profitability by using every opportunity to improve business processes.	1	2	3	4
Organizes own work to stay on track toward targets, keeping others informed of progress or barriers to achievement.	1	2	3	4
Creates a team identity by developing a shared vision, mission, and goals jointly with the team.	1	2	3	4
Works toward creating practical, innovative solutions to issues.	1	2	3	4
Deals with complex, sometimes ambiguous information, revising priorities as necessary.	1	2	3	4
Foresees and influences change by maintaining a positive attitude to new ideas and new ways of doing things.	1	2	3	4
Delivers consistent messages that reinforce the organization's priorities.	1	2	3	4
Provides a clear sense of direction for the team and co-workers.	1	2	3	4
Total for Strategist Add the numbers you circled in each column and record the sum in the box for that column.				
Add the scores in the four boxes for your Strategist competency score.				

Champion	Works to achieve results and improve individual and organizational goals.			
Behaviors *Please rate yourself in the following criteria areas*	1 = low		4 = high	
Personifies high standards of honesty, integrity, trust, openness, fairness, and compassion.	1	2	3	4
Assumes own responsibility for developing leadership competencies and management skills to meet individual performance targets.	1	2	3	4
Adapts behavior and work methods to changing conditions and unexpected obstacles.	1	2	3	4
Seriously considers feedback from others on existing ideas, procedures, and policies, seeking out creative/innovative solutions for improvement.	1	2	3	4
Produces sound conclusions and recommendations that contribute to effective decision making.	1	2	3	4
Takes ownership for areas of responsibility.	1	2	3	4
Uses resources efficiently.	1	2	3	4
Initiates action and provides support and systems to achieve goals.	1	2	3	4
Understands personal strengths and limitations.	1	2	3	4
Commits to action and is decisive as a situation demands.	1	2	3	4
Total for Champion Add the numbers you circled in each column and record the sum in the box for that column.				
Add the scores in the four boxes for your Champion competency score.				

Enabler	Shares information/ideas clearly and listens for understanding to promote work relationships.			

Behaviors *Please rate yourself in the following criteria areas*	1 = low 4 = high			
Confronts conflict constructively to minimize impact on self, others, and the organization.	1	2	3	4
Shares information and expertise with others to increase understanding and informed decision making.	1	2	3	4
Inspires and encourages others to do their best by providing meaningful, constructive feedback and encouragement.	1	2	3	4
Fosters collaboration and exchange of ideas with others from diverse backgrounds, experiences, and functions.	1	2	3	4
Helps people reflect and learn from previous experiences to avoid future pitfalls.	1	2	3	4
Actively contributes individual expertise and experience to achieve team goals.	1	2	3	4
Provides information and exchange of ideas in a way that promotes open and candid communication and understanding.	1	2	3	4
Encourages open discussion of differences of opinion and controversial issues through impartial questioning and clarification that is directed toward a positive outcome.	1	2	3	4
Maintains the self-confidence and self-esteem of others, respecting cross-cultural and diverse perspectives.	1	2	3	4
Motivates others to achieve desired outcomes by directing, coaching, and delegating as the situation requires.	1	2	3	4
Total for Enabler Add the numbers you circled in each column and record the sum in the box for that column.				
Add the scores in the four boxes for your Enabler competency score.				

Lao-Tsu, the father of Taoism, said, "The way to do is to be" (verse 47 in *The Way of Life According to Lao Tsu*, translated by Witter Bynner). Leaders who have achieved outstanding success across the world score high in each of the ABL role categories below. These high scores demonstrate their capacity and willingness to function as an ABL because it is our belief that you must "do to be." If you are interested in determining if you have the traits of an ABL, answer the questions in each of the preceding four tables and total your scores for each section. Following this assessment, we will explain the ABL model in further detail.

ABL MODEL

As mentioned earlier, Agile Business Leadership is more than a mindset; it is a set of roles, traits, and competencies focused on organizational and individual components. These traits are crucial for every leader in every culture and in every industry. When we talked to Australian leaders working in the Philippines, they said, "It's challenging to work in this country because of all the corruption involved and the requirement for doing business." When we talked to U.S. leaders working in a controversial startup, they said, "Traditional organizations are a bunch of babies and need to realize that things are going to change and we plan to make sure of that." When we talked to leaders in the Middle East, they said, "As with all things in the Middle East, relationship building is 80 percent of the game and things just slow down due to various factors—bureaucracy, ego, heat, and communication." When we talked with leaders in Costa Rica, they said, "We were having so much trouble getting work done and communicating what we wanted. Then we learned that the word 'dialogue' in Spanish means 'to argue', and began to realize why none of the workers wanted to 'dialogue' with us to resolve the issues." When we talked with leaders in Denmark about working with people in the United States, they said, "Why are people being so polite in this meeting? Get to the point, be direct, and stop apologizing and saying thank you all the time." When we talked with telecommunication leaders in Paris, France, they told us they must strategize differently because "the market force is evaporating and changing because there are less and less customers due to large communication companies buying smaller ones and putting them out of business and this makes the market smaller."

It's easy to understand why it is a challenge for successful leaders to work in a global economy. Not only must they "follow the sun" while doing business, they must meet the requirements of their industry and culture. There is an enormous amount of factors to take into consideration when leading with an organization. The ABL model is a performance model providing the bedrock of required skills and abilities for any leader who wants to positively impact success. This model has its underpinnings in the idea of social and emotional intelligence, since it involves an ability to manage oneself in the context of interpersonal relations. In other words, to be an effective leader one must be able to perform a task with an appropriate level of interpersonal skills, professional knowledge, and operational ability to achieve the goal. These ABL components can be driven from both internal and external sources. The model emphasizes self-awareness, engagement techniques, knowledge, and methods for business development. The ABL model is deceptively simple. It answers the question, "What type of leadership is needed in the current world of business?"

When developing this model we drew from our work with clients from around the world. A theory emerged as we helped to provide clients

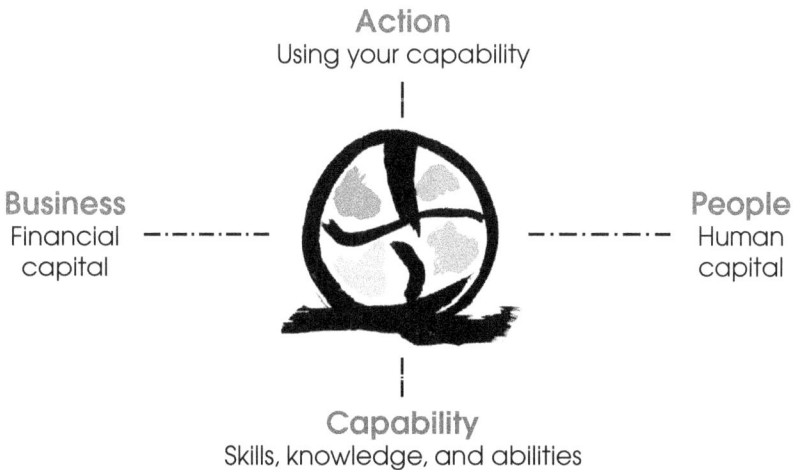

Action
Using your capability

Business
Financial
capital

People
Human
capital

Capability
Skills, knowledge, and abilities

with a meaningful description for which types of elements are needed by a leader in today's emerging markets. This model offers concepts that have stood the test of time and that we believe are equally relevant for the tough challenges that lie ahead.

Agile Business Leaders consistently and successfully face two realities:

i) The need to be business- AND people-focused and
ii) The expectation that they build personal and organizational competencies AND achieve action

THE HORIZONTAL REALITY

A reality for leaders is working with i) Business (financial capital—wealth employed for the production of more wealth) and ii) People (human capital—the sum total of an organization's human performance capability). The horizontal line of this model addresses the factors impacting the success of an organization.

Business includes: assets, liabilities, and equity. It includes the money, securities, property, and other valuables that collectively represent the wealth of the business and are used to generate income by investing in either a business or different income sources. Business capital is the net worth of a business or in simpler terms, the amount by which the organization's assets exceed its liabilities. The Business side of this model also includes the mission, goals, values, and vision for the organization. It includes the methods and practices an organization endorses to achieve financial well-being.

People includes: the collective human resources of the organization that contribute to organizational performance. An organization's human capital is the collective sum of the attributes, life experience, knowledge, inventiveness, energy, and enthusiasm that its people choose to invest in their work. It incorporates the group dynamics, values,

Business		People
Financial capital	Agility	Human capital

norms, attitudes, motivational forces, and collaboration. It is the organization's human ecosystem, or more simply put, the personality of the organization. The People side is the accumulated present value of the employees. It is the component of the organization that drives the organization and influences strategic operations, employee loyalty, and commitment.

THE VERTICAL REALITY

Another reality of Capabilities (an individual's unique knowledge, skills, and abilities) and Action (turning talent into effective responses) addresses the components of character and behavior.

Action includes: the ability to transform knowledge and talent into actions. Action involves sensing changes in signals from the environment (both internal and external) and the ability to adapt accordingly. In addition, it includes developing and communicating strategic initiatives, adapting current operations to improve effectiveness, implementing new business directions, motivating people to achieve results, and aligning oneself around the direction of the organization. The Action side of this model also includes the methods and practices an organization needs to create, capture, transfer, and mobilize knowledge to enable the organization to adapt to a changing environment.

Capability includes: the sum of the individual's knowledge, skills, and attributes. Capability focuses on the uniqueness of the individual and

Action
Using your capability

Agility

Capability
Skills, knowledge, and abilities

his or her expertise, natural aptitude, acquired proficiency, and capacity to perform. Capability refers to both a person's ability to learn in the future and actions that he or she can do now. It incorporates consistent behavior and a degree of mental capacity and moral quality.

These two realities—Business & People and Action & Capability—can be used to form a model for understanding the roles, traits, and competencies needed to be an Agile Business Leader.

When the two realities are crossed, four quadrants are created to define the four roles of an Agile Business Leader: (1) Strategist, (2) Enabler, (3) Champion, and (4) Specialist. Each of these roles comes with a list of traits and competencies associated with them. Our thinking is that a leader must have ALL traits in order to be effective.

A CALL FOR CHANGE IN LEADERSHIP STYLES

The Agile Business Leader approach will make a profound contribution to any organization through the process of rapid and effective organizational learning and through building leadership agility.

Agility is about adaptability, responsiveness, innovation, and learning. Agile Business Leadership is all about the release of human possibilities for quickly, efficiently, and effectively responding to the needs of the customer.

Competitive advantage can be generated by a speed-to-market approach or it can also be created through an organization's ability to accelerate the development of its leadership talent. By efficiently developing the best leadership skills and competencies, organizations can extend their competitive advantage in the market and drive enterprise-wide performance and sustainable growth for the organization.

In competency terms, an Agile Business Leader should be able to develop and communicate a strategic vision, implement new business directions, and motivate people to achieve results and align themselves around a clearly articulated strategy. To accomplish this list of criteria, ABLs must be skillful problem solvers and coaches, adept at developing high-performance collaborative teams, and able to impact decisions within and outside of their organization.

By promoting the development of Agile Business Leaders, we are calling for a shift that requires an increased level of adaptability and flexibility in business operations. We are challenging organizations to find ways to support this model and ensure that individuals receive the training and support needed to address business demands in this globally connected, hyperactive environment.

As change in business is inevitable, the traits and competencies of the ABL provide the capacity to ensure survival and oversee the dynamic growth of an organization. All ABL roles, traits, and competencies are essential to enable leaders to quickly deal with and adapt to change. The ABL's capacity can be taught, learned, monitored, and measured.

The best organizations, whether they know it or not, develop agile leaders who leverage the knowledge and wisdom of the organization through their role as Enabler, Champion, Specialist, and Strategist as the individual situation requires.

2

THE STRATEGIST

❖ *Navigates the Course* ❖

I am not afraid of storms for I am learning how to sail my ship.

LOUISA MAY ALCOTT
American author, *Little Women* (1868)

I n the role of Strategist, a leader responds to the realities of needing to be business-focused and at the same time needing to achieve action. The Strategist is focused on helping the business grow and mobilizing and transforming people to make that happen.

The four traits of the Strategist are

❐ Change Leadership
❐ Strategic Adaptability
❐ Resources for Innovation
❐ Path to More Profitability

In the role of Strategist, the ABL understands reality and expects that things may not go as planned, thriving on unplanned opportunities and creating the future by visualizing it. The Strategist is intuitive, with a vision based on ethical business values, and is always asking, "What's next?" "Where else?" and "Why not?" Because of this inquisitive nature, the Strategist helps create a sense of identity for people in the organization by galvanizing followers and keeping interest and motivation high. A Strategist is a big thinker whose actions are dynamic and daring: the Strategist seeks large gains and is not afraid to take smart, calculated risks. A Strategist can manage a housing crisis, a commercial crisis, an economic crisis, or an employment crisis because of being a quantum-leap thinker who can convince followers to discard their policy and procedures manuals and create commonsense, flexible, and ethical guidelines. The Strategist helps design an organization's infrastructure to support every aspect of innovation by helping to create or modify the organization's collective values, beliefs, attitudes, and behaviors. The Strategist knows that the complex choices in the business world today are not the same as the choices that had to be made long ago. Taking all components into consideration and putting all the origins of business aside, the Strategist focuses on generating business and cash for the organization by acting decisively.

THE NEED FOR STRATEGISTS

A volatile and intensely competitive marketplace demands high-energy, quick, and agile leaders with resilient teams comprising people who can translate their strengths into competitive advantage. This world of breathtaking, rapid change, combined with global transportability of goods and services, means businesses (buyers and sellers) are able to exchange information and demand services more instantaneously and inexpensively than ever before. Leaders who can strategize in a systematic way expose reality and act on it. They take on the role of organization systems architects and contribute decisively to critical areas and tasks.

Leaders who think about an organization as a whole system create a strategic plan that is aligned to the final goal. The leader

- Builds value.
- Creates cultures of accountability.
- Establishes practices to recruit, retain, develop, and motivate people.
- Transforms profitability and performance.
- Manages customer-value creation.
- Enhances the product portfolio.
- Designs joint go-to-market approaches.
- Recognizes when a project is capital-intensive.

THE AGILE STRATEGY IS MORE THAN THINKING

Leaders typically strategize on

- Creating revenue retention.
- Managing risks and mitigations.
- Designing proposals for becoming a market maker.

These same leaders might feel they are not unique because of many other leaders doing the same tasks. Agile Business Leaders recognize that they might be outnumbered, but they have confidence that they will not be outsmarted because of their agility and ability to respond quickly to the reality that faces them. Their strategic plan incorporates a level of thinking that includes

• Not making assumptions about the industry.
• Realistically assessing the organization's capabilities.
• Appropriately linking organizational strategy to business operations and to the people implementing the strategy.

- Carefully synchronizing people from different disciplines to create a well-rounded approach for the future.
- Openly linking rewards to outcomes.
- Continuously changing assumptions as the environment changes.
- Constantly upgrading the company's capabilities to meet the challenges of an ambitious strategy.

A typical leader draws from everyone's strengths, talents, and abilities and defines the parameters of an organization's vision for the future. Sadly, this typical leader only addresses half of the equation for strategic success, meaning that the strategy is only half as good as it could be. The ABL Strategist not only incorporates the key factors of strategic planning—including defining business success and incorporating functional requirements—but also brings the plan to life. The ABL has the ability to implement the strategic plan.

Some leaders might want to achieve their strategic plan, but they do not have the ability or knowledge to leverage the organization's assets to implement and deliver the plan. Implementation involves discussing the hows, the whos, and the whats of the plan and determining how to propel the plan forward. Implementing a strategic plan is about

- Questioning assumptions.
- Mandating tenacious follow-through.
- Ensuring accountability of everyone involved.
- Thinking of ways to optimize performance.
- Engaging the workforce to be more productive, profitable, safe, customer-focused, and innovative.

Agile Business Leaders make their presence felt in business by leading the strategic plan while implementing and generating actions and results.

IMPLEMENTING FOR RESULTS

The Strategist does not stand on a mountaintop, thinking strategically and attempting to inspire people. Instead, heart and soul are immersed in the organization, with a desire to implement a positive, focused strategy. Strategists are engaged personally and deeply in the business, its people, and the industry, incorporating rigor, intensity, and depth as they take account of people and operational realities. Positive results emerge from this approach.

A strategy is only as good as its implementation. Today's business world is so fluid and volatile that many leaders are ultimately forced to admit, "The plan that was supposed to happen . . . didn't." In our view, an organization cannot rely on one strategy or firmly believe that it alone will provide the ultimate solution or direction. Rather, the leader's critical tasks are to

- Help make the organization capable of implementing and adjusting the strategic plan.
- Respond quickly to business challenges.
- Face the business environment with an open mind.

Strategic leaders must give the utmost attention to ensure that an organization's strategy (1) is created realistically, (2) is implemented ambitiously, and (3) incorporates all the information at hand about the markets, resources, and relationships.

STRATEGIST TRAITS AND COMPETENCIES

Strategists develop their traits through seven competencies:

Change Leadership:
1. Create and communicate vision and values.
2. Promote change.

Strategic Adaptability:
3. Think strategically.
4. Develop strategic solutions.

Resources for Innovation:
5. Recognize and rectify specific inefficiencies.
6. Resolve issues through innovation.

Path to More Profitability:
7. Ensure good ideas come to fruition.

STRATEGIST TRAIT

#1

◢ CHANGE LEADERSHIP ▽

**We all have big changes in our lives that
are more or less a second chance.**

HARRISON FORD
Actor

We assume by now you have heard throughout your career that change is inevitable in any organization. What we would like to stress is that how a leader deals with change is often the differentiator between a successful and a non-successful leader. During the change process, the Strategist is focused on results rather than methods, systems, and procedures. The Strategist puts efforts toward aligning the beliefs and values of people with the overall goals and vision of the organization, and the methods and systems take shape and adjust from there.

If organizations are to make radical changes, ones that will project them at warp speed ahead of their competitors, it will be because of their dedicated, passionate, and agile leaders who think and act boldly. Strategists with the competency of Change Leadership are referred to as

- Lead agents of change.
- Facilitators of change.
- Enablers of change.
- Interpreters.
- Master communicators.
- Promoters of change.
- Resisters of the status quo.

The Strategist knows that change can improve output and protect an organization from sluggish growth.

Types of Change

We believe change in organizations can be classified in different ways and is usually classified under one of four types:

Anticipatory Changes: Planned changes based on expected situations.

Reactive Changes: Changes made in response to unexpected situations.

Incremental Changes: Subsystem adjustments required to keep the organization on course.

Strategic Changes: Altering the overall shape or direction of the organization.

Through any change process, the Strategist helps people understand the purposes of the change, critical targets that need to be met, and best approaches for responding positively to the situation.

Dealing with the Greatest Challenge to Change

One of the greatest challenges inherent in any change initiative is ensuring the retention of new behaviors. We have seen it all too often when companies create a plan for change and implement the beginning of the change process yet cannot implement a complete and sustainable change where people think, act, and behave differently.

It's too easy for people to fall back into old familiar habits soon after a change has been undertaken. We have heard new clients say, "Oh, we did a change process a couple of years ago, and it was good for about three months and then everything went back to how it usually was." When we work with clients, we do not call a three-month shift in behavior a *change*. We call this brief switch a *disruption*. The Strategist models the appropriate behavior desired of staff and looks closely at what behaviors are being supported and rewarded at all levels. Although it might not be preferred, the Strategist takes time to listen and respond to the concerns of people and provides the necessary resources for the changes to become reliable and sustainable.

The Organization as a System

To promote and lead people through change while being agile in the approach to Change Leadership, leaders should first consider thinking about the organization as an entire system. This is also known as Systems Thinking, and the concept is not new. In 1990, Peter Senge wrote a book about Systems Thinking entitled *The Fifth Discipline: The Art and Practice of the Learning Organization*. In his book, Senge suggests five learning disciplines necessary to cultivate thinking in an organization. The following five points briefly summarize his theory and provide some quotes from Senge's book.

a. Building Shared Vision: Any time you change something, you are proposing something new. Even if the change is better, the natural tendency is to resist or ignore it until someone helps us see the destination more clearly and we warm up to the significance of being there. This is the work of a good vision. *"If any one idea about leadership has inspired organizations for thousands of years, it's the capacity to hold a shared picture of the future we seek to create"* (p. 9).

b. Mental Models (beliefs, values, mindsets, and assumptions that dictate the way we think and act): Mental models are the biggest barrier to successful change and one of the keys to unlocking its secrets. To a large extent, thinking controls our actions and behavior. *"Mental models are deeply ingrained assumptions, generalizations, or even pictures or images that influence how we understand the world and how we take action"* (p. 8). Mental models offer the biggest leverage point for leaders looking to create deep and self-sustaining change.

c. Personal Mastery: To change things on the outside, leaders often need to first make definitive changes from within. These changes often need to come before any organizational changes they may want to make. It is one thing to get others to change, but can we successfully change ourselves? This discipline has to do with personal work and *"continually clarifying and deepening our per-*

sonal vision, of focusing our energies, of developing patience, and of seeing reality objectively" (p. 7).

d. Team Learning: Change typically happens when a team starts to *think together* and develop the critical reflection, inquiry, and discussion skills needed to conduct more focused conversations that lead to better decisions and common commitments to action. *"Team learning is vital because teams, not individuals, are the fundamental learning unit in modern organizations"* (p. 10). Team learning enables groups of people to look for the larger picture that lies beyond individual perspectives. This type of discipline in dialogue also involves learning how to recognize the patterns of interaction in teams that undermine learning.

e. Systems Thinking: Systems Thinking acts as a unifier for the other four disciplines. It is a framework for seeing interrelationships rather than just things. Systems Thinking is the discipline required to understand, manage, and sustain change. It enables us to better see the interrelationships that underlie complex change situations rather than only seeing simplistic (and inaccurate) linear cause-effect chains. Systems Thinking serves to make the results of the other disciplines work together for business benefit. Without the Systems Thinking discipline, processes can be put in place to solve short-term and individual problems, but they will cause bigger problems somewhere else in the system. According to Senge, *"The cornerstone of any learning organization is the fifth Discipline—systems thinking. Without systems thinking each of the disciplines would be isolated . . . The fifth discipline integrates them to form the whole system . . .*

> Systems thinking needs the disciplines of building shared vision, mental models, and personal mastery to realize its potential. Building shared vision fosters a commitment to the long term. Mental models focus on the openness needed to unearth shortcomings in our present ways of seeing the world. Team learning develops the skills of groups of people

to look for the larger picture that lies beyond individual perspectives. And personal mastery fosters the personal motivation to continually learn how our actions affect our world.
Lastly, systems thinking makes understandable the subtlest
aspect of the learning organization—the new way individuals perceive themselves and their world. At the heart of a
learning organization is a shift of mind—from seeing ourselves as separate from the world to connected to the world,
from seeing problems as caused by someone or something
'out there' to seeing how our own actions create the problems we experience. (p. 12)

According to Senge, leaders in organizations learn to thrive on change
and constantly innovate by methodically cultivating these five disciplines. Senge points out, *"These might just as well be called the leadership disciplines as the learning disciplines. Those who excel in these areas will be the natural leaders of learning organizations. Ultimately,
people follow people who believe in something and have the abilities to
achieve results in the service of those beliefs. Or, to put it another way,
who are the natural leaders of learning organizations? They are the
learners"* (p. 360).

An Organization Is a System

If you think of an organization as a system, then it becomes a set of integrated and mutually dependent parts. When the organizational system works well, all the parts interact in a way that produces a unified
and exceptional flow of information, energy, and materials. A high-
functioning *system* or organization continually exchanges information
and feedback among its various parts and ensures all components remain closely aligned and focused on achieving the common goal of the
organization. If any area in the system seems weak or misaligned, then
the system makes the necessary adjustments to ensure the goals are
achieved.

We compare a well-run organizational system to a racing yacht. The
organization can pull into port, race through rising seas, manage the

winds of change, and stay on course to reach its final destination. The yacht is *not* the only factor affecting the voyage. There are many other factors at play.

The mystery question about yachting is, why is it that one yacht and crew among dozens of identical yachts can come out on top in an ocean race? This answer is linked to a sophisticated system that by necessity must operate in harmony to be successful.

As in any system, there are many factors involved in getting the racing yacht to perform. The picture above illustrates such an operation. The yacht has the capacity to deliver high performance, yet if it is pushed too hard in adverse conditions, it will break. The crew must seize opportunities, take risks, and overcome the challenges and constraints. If the crew is not reliable or the right partnerships have not been formed, then the yacht might never leave the port or might get left to sink at sea.

Barry remembers back in school when he was asked by a friend in his class to go sailing. The friend's name was Doug Trott. Doug actually went on to win many championships in sailing, and Barry is quite sure that Doug's experience of sailing with him on this particular day had absolutely nothing to do with Doug's excellence in the sport!

DOUG TOOK ME OUT ON HIS SABOT, a piece of timber just big enough to hold two kids and a bed sheet, but boy did that thing fly! What Doug didn't tell me that day was that we were actually sailing in a competition and that he was the reigning champion. His regular buddy had gotten sick, so I was asked as a fill-in. I had never been in a sailing boat before, so he gave me a few quick instructions on what to do and where to sit, and we were off. I remember being quite excited to see that we were soon out in front and going like the wind. Then there was a slight hiccup in the system—me! Doug's order to "let out the sheet" drew an immediate response from his new and excited crewman, except I pulled the rope tighter instead of letting it out. Now these little boats really do go fast, which makes the controls very sensitive to the slightest error. Apparently tightening the sail was not just a small error, and the inevitable happened. We were upside down in a nano-second. We righted the boat, but it was half-full of water, which slowed us down considerably. We didn't win that day, and Doug never asked me to help out again. In fairness, he did take me out for "fun," but that was to be my last competition.

Like yachts, organizational systems can be explained as having

- The ability to deal with the environment in which we are sailing (the inputs to this system).
- A skipper (a leader) and a team with a clearly articulated strategy (guiding coalition).
- A good crew (people with aligned values, knowledge, and experience).
- A capable yacht (a structure that supports the crew, including having everyone know what needs to be done and what their role in the system is).

- Relationships and interactions (the behavior shown and a dynamic allowing for conflicts to be resolved quickly and positively with innovation, creativity, and excellent communications).
- Great race results (the output resulting in a sustainable, profitable business and motivated, energized, and increased performance from the crew).

The Winds of Change

Flexible and adaptive organizations, like yachts, have rationally designed systems and are deliberately structured and restructured to improve their output capacity. The entire organization must be in concert to perform well. The Strategist must scrutinize the environment carefully and understand it well. He or she must examine everything, including economic and demographic trends, regulatory shifts in new technologies, alliances between competitors, and the drivers of increasing or decreasing demand for the organization's products and services. It is the Agile Business Leader who synchronizes all of the organization's components and links them with a strategy for change within a context of the shifting political atmosphere, the social environment, and the macroeconomics (behavior of the economy as a whole for forecasting economic conditions). The Strategist exercises all personal disciplines and innovation to deal with the ever-present unanticipated events that occur.

We suggest the following list of eight factors as influences on an organization/yacht. As with any influence or change, there are potential pluses and minuses that can occur in the rough waters of change. For each of the factors we list the key areas of focus for a leader to be concerned with, and how a leader and his or her followers might negatively view the situation.

1. Environment

Key Focus: External market, technology, competitors, suppliers, real estate, community, labor market, inflation rate, government regulations and taxes, cultural and social trends, and the price and availability of natural resources.

Negative reactions when organization/yacht is rocked by change: Business survival perceived at risk, government regulations force adoption of new systems, customers become more fearful, costs rise and prices stay flat, organization's skills and resources seen as limiting what alternatives can be considered, emerging economic and market trends turn into business threats and missed opportunities.

Positive benefit to changing conditions: Opportunities to locate new supportive environments, understand what the markets and regulators need, increase clarity on business environment, analyze competition, create clarity on brand differentiation, match the core competencies to produce a competitive advantage, diversify portfolio by adding new enterprises or products, create self-regulatory initiatives.

2. Input

Key Focus: Materials, talent, financial investment, equipment, resources, raw goods, laws, regulations.

Negative reactions when organization/yacht is rocked by change: Inadequate analysis, inadequate information. Lack of internal integration, lack of "fit" between input and outcome.

Positive benefit to changing conditions: Coordination of resources, adequate analysis made, clarity of purpose and outcome, alignment to organization's mission, assurance of gathering proper resources.

3. Partnership

Key Focus: Consists of the network of individuals within and around an organization that most influences the mission and goals of the organization. It maintains an influence on goals through informal, rather than formal, channels.

Negative reactions when organization/yacht is rocked by change: Sabotaging outcomes, concerned with survival, wants personal needs met not organizational needs, negative influence on behavioral standards, and leverages relationship power to in-formally influence goals. Outside forces exert a great deal of influ-ence on organization, and lack of access to physical resources, capital, possession of tacit knowledge, or access to individuals with vital information, competing commitments (change can dis-rupt employees in their pursuit of other goals).

Positive benefit to changing conditions: Support and pursue the stated goals, conversion in the current status quo of relationships within the organization, maintain values such as compassion, community service, and stewardship, improves morale, teamwork.

4. Structure

Key Focus: The way people are organized in relation to each other and to the workflow. Structure includes definition of departments, units and levels of supervision, job/work design, span of supervi-sory control, delegation of authority, physical layout, business planning, information/communication, human resources (for ex-ample, compensation, promotion, performance evaluation), evalua-tion, resource allocation, template for achievement, compen-sation, career development, succession and planning.

Negative reactions when organization/yacht is rocked by change: Lack of internal integration, non-helpfulness, dehumani-zation, false professionalism, bureaucratization and stratification, undue focus on unapplied knowledge and information, threat to job status/security. Employees worry that any change may threaten their job or security. Leaders need to understand how the system functions and where and how often errors occur. Important fac-tors must be accounted for, including hiring, firing, training, con-trolling, planning, scheduling, compensating, reporting, etc.

Positive benefit to changing conditions: Profitability and cost-effectiveness: improving, creating, and tracking implementation and outcomes; developing systems for high-end outcomes; and creating awareness of essential competencies and skills.

5. Reliability

Key Focus: Supportive and consistent actions by all involved in the organization.

Negative reactions when organization/yacht is rocked by change: Breakdown in peer support, no self-responsibility, environmental hazards, stress, exploitation, lack of coping skills, low self-esteem and group support.

Positive benefit to changing conditions: Providing a professional identity, mobilizing organizational support factors, teamwork/communication, colleague and associate relations, objective setting and leadership commitment, bringing reality into the open, inclusive dialogues.

6. Culture

Key Focus: Norms of the organization, the "way we do things around here." Culture is reflected in people's behavior and language. Culture is a product of group experience and is found where there is a definable group with some history. It is what forms shared assumptions and the meaning a group gives to symbolic systems, artifacts, values, routines, informal norms/rules of conduct, habits, and traditions. Leadership behavior shapes a culture.

Negative reactions when organization/yacht is rocked by change: Challenges to basic assumptions, contested interpretation, political gamesmanship, denial, make excuses, take action to avoid being blamed, punished, or harmed.

Positive benefit to changing conditions: Achieving sustained and positive results, improved customer and consumer relations, changing principles, people embracing reality and engaging in constructive debates.

7. People

Key Focus: Types of professions, knowledge and skills of the people in the organization and those needed to do the work. It is also the need, potential, and resources/methodologies for skill and capability development.

Negative reactions when organization/yacht is rocked by change: Resistance, fear, political positioning, frustration, anger, conflict.

Positive benefit to changing conditions: Releasing potential—changes in the goals would cause changes in the behaviors and expectations of managers.

8. Productivity

Key Focus: Economic, technological, communal, and financial soundness. End result achievement, value as a long-term investment, good use of corporate assets, innovativeness, ability to attract and retain employees.

Negative reactions when organization/yacht is rocked by change: Employees often don't know what happens when change is introduced into this mix, overemphasis on activities and a lack of attention to results, prevention of capitalization.

Positive benefit to changing conditions: Financial soundness, internal integration, performance/excellence, increased production, cost reduction, increased sales, increased earnings, reduced turnover, worker productivity and profitability, return on investment, legislative victories, and raised public awareness.

Change within a organizational system involves a change in the ideas, points of view, and habits of many people (those inside and outside the yacht) with strong convictions and prejudices. Systems can only be improved to the extent that everyone who works in them understands how they work. We are constantly helping our clients to rethink their organizations and view each of them as a whole system. We encourage leaders to create meaning, purpose, community, and profit.

The ABL Strategist positions a competitive yacht with an effective crew to achieve success. A strategic-minded leader may not be able to control the weather, but can design a ship, equip it with a crew that can navigate the ocean under all weather and environmental conditions, and help people yearn for the far and endless sea. Even with the latest and greatest systems and processes, an organization's performance is limited severely without the cooperative attitudes and support of the organization's culture. You cannot separate structure from behavior any more than you can separate economics and technology from people. If someone on the yacht does not know some aspect of sailing or how the crew should operate, it could be a very rough ride for all, particularly in rough waters when you need "all hands on deck."

The point we are trying to make here is that an organization's performance—like a yacht's—must be directly linked to the attitudes of its people (its crew). This means that traditional leaders must move from a problem-solving approach for strategizing to a more systems improvement approach. It means moving from using an expert solutions approach and moving toward involving everybody in the system.

The Reality of Change

In Change Leadership, the Strategist tackles high-leverage solutions by changing things that lead to lasting significant improvement (while using a minimum amount of effort). This type of leader incorporates Change Leadership by ensuring

- Everyone in the organization understands the big picture.
- Systems are in place to show that employees are valued and recognized for their effort and impact.
- Desired new behaviors are rewarded.
- Customers are satisfied and therefore loyal.

In the role of Strategist, the leader sees value of change because without change the organization would become stagnant. The Strategist knows that change can help organizations grow, heal, repair, develop, and expand. Unfortunately when it comes to change, the reality is that the value of change often meets resistance, is misunderstood, or is ignored.

People generally resist change of any kind because it disrupts the ritual and order in their lives. In our work we typically find people resist change because of

- **Emotional Side Effects:** Forced acceptance of change creates a sense of powerlessness, anger, and passive resistance to that change.
- **Lack of Trust in Leadership:** Promises of improvement are not met and communications from the top are not believed because employees do not trust leadership to be able to deliver on promises.
- **Fear of Failure:** Intimidation caused by change and doubt is created because people believe they do not have the ability to meet new challenges.
- **Personality Conflicts:** Employees dislike the leader and his or her style or approach.
- **Poor Timing:** Other events counter the planned change, and people conspire and create resentment to the change.
- **Lack of Leadership Interpersonal Skills:** The leader is oblivious or lacks empathy or sensitivity to people's views about change.

Overcoming Resistance and Changing for Improvement

The Strategist knows that when it comes to change, the consequences of inaction are often worse than action. Therefore, getting people on board can only have positive results. To overcome resistance, the Strategist engages people within the organizational system by stating the *corporate imperative*: "Change is going to happen and it needs to happen because . . ." The Strategist helps people realize that the best way to view change is as a dynamic expedition and not as a laid-back destination.

Economic developments over the coming decade will accelerate changes as well as the expectations for business leaders to be agile enough to take advantage of them. Greater competition as a result of globalization and the rise of the knowledge economy has created an important need for leaders to be able to have the trait of Change Leadership. Agile Business Leaders consider new, irregular, and evolving challenges as a way to be more agile in learning, adapting, and enabling solutions to be created.

The Strategist makes changes for improvement by promoting a high level of adaptability and flexibility in business operations. Although the need for Change Leadership is not new, the ability to change at least as quickly as the marketplace has become critical to the success of an organization's future sustainability. You cannot change what you do not acknowledge. Strategists are clear about what they want and take charge of making it happen. As a leader the Strategist

- Provides direction.
- Sets an example.
- Motivates through inspiration.
- Builds teams based on respect and trust.
- Values change.

The change we are talking about in this trait is inevitably linked to changing oneself. Change or be changed.

Strategists

- Stay open minded and adjust to the situation if necessary.
- Anticipate change.
- Adapt quickly and effectively to what needs to be done.
- Constantly look for better ways of doing everything.
- Maintain authenticity in their interactions and communications.

Leveraging the Benefits of Change

At the heart of Change Leadership is the ability to link people, strategy, and operations. This is the foundation for conceiving and executing a strategy for change. It is the Strategist who minimizes the negative impacts of change and promotes and leverages the positive opportunities and benefits of change.

The list below provides a selection of tactics that can help leverage change and maximize its benefits:

- Foster an innovative mindset.
- Encourage feedback.
- Deepen the sense of organizational purpose.
- Create a culture and systems that encourage and value change.
- Build team spirit.
- Encourage problem solving rather than avoidance.
- Supplement formal authority with knowledge and skill-based authority.

- Increase accountability for planning and implementing.
- Resist limiting yourself by what you think is possible.
- Focus on the specific result and not on the process.
- Experience and describe a goal as if it is in the present tense.
- Increase the willingness for people to take calculated risks.

The Change Leadership Question

Leaders who successfully execute change have rigor and intensity. The list above supports the competencies of the Strategist and our thinking about gaining skills in Change Leadership. Leaders with these abilities can establish a sustainable balance within their environment and can understand that people, processes, and strategy must be in harmony and focused on one vision. A leader with these abilities can easily answer the question, "When thinking about change, how can I leverage 'the system' to achieve change?"

STRATEGIST TRAIT

#2

STRATEGIC ADAPTABILITY

It is not the strongest of the species that survives, nor the most intelligent that survives. It is the one that is the most adaptable to change.

CHARLES DARWIN

For this competency we focus on the leader having a flexible, anticipatory mindset. Being adaptable is one of the best foundations to build upon because it offers a perspective that allows for possibilities that may not be visible from a crisis or an expansive "seascape" (again going back to the organization as a yacht analogy). The ability to be flexible and highly adaptive requires an attitude of openness and a willingness to embrace an opportunity rather than a mindset that is dominated by problems and fears. When we talk about Strategic Adaptability in this competency, we are referring to the leader having the ability to change at least as quickly as the marketplace.

The Structure of Strategy

Creating a strategy is an everyday, continuous, and adaptive process. It requires ideas about how markets can be won and how organizations can be operated. It requires values that everyone understands and can live up to. It requires energy for stretching the boundaries and being passionate about implementation. It requires thinking about new organizational structures and morphing the business into new levels.

Every strategy must clearly lay out the specifics of the anatomy of the business. It must emphasize how the business will make money, today and in the future. We find ourselves always reminding clients that the essential component to every strategic plan is an understanding of the business drivers, resources available, speed to market, revenue growth, market share, and competitive advantage. How a leader adapts strategic thinking to address business sustainability during times of change is a vital competency to the Agile Business Leader.

Strategies for the Future

The Strategist knows that organizations do not exist in a vacuum; they are continually affected in numerous ways by change. The Strategist also knows that people have different approaches and types of thinking when it comes to strategizing for change and growth:

- Change comes from outside the world the individual works in. Strategic thinking should incorporate stretched thinking and perspectives of different industries.
- People are inherently able to change and develop. Strategic thinking should be considered a natural process.
- People can change other people's views about change and growth with the right incentives. Strategic thinking includes rewards and punishments as part of the long-term plan.

- A person's views about change are determined by how a person constructs and understands the situation from his or her personal beliefs. Strategic thinking should involve inclusion and cover communication.
- Yesterday's remedies often create tomorrow's problems. Strategic thinking should consider the past as it moves toward the future.

All of these perspectives are valid and may need some expanded response in the new global world of business. If we consider how organizations and strategic leaders acted on change in the past, we find they did not worry too much about the enormous impact or size the external environment played on the strategic process. Today strategic thinking needs to change. Now external forces are considered with much more respect, and leaders know they play a much more important role in strategic thinking.

Most of the organizations we work with believe that they have little or no influence or control over the economic, social, political, technological, and environmental factors in their external environment. They

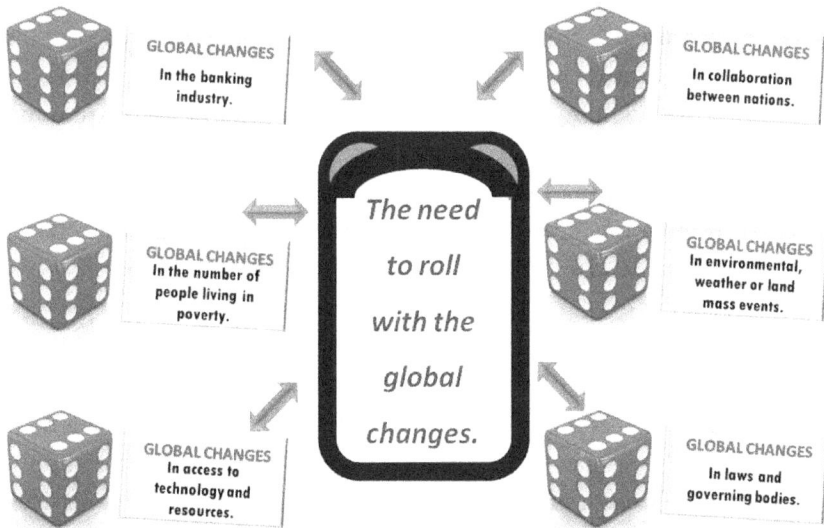

GLOBAL CHANGES
In the banking industry.

GLOBAL CHANGES
In collaboration between nations.

GLOBAL CHANGES
In the number of people living in poverty.

The need to roll with the global changes.

GLOBAL CHANGES
In environmental, weather or land mass events.

GLOBAL CHANGES
In access to technology and resources.

GLOBAL CHANGES
In laws and governing bodies.

Changes Through Strategic Adaptability

tend to focus more on their organization or on the specific industry they know. We suggest leaders reconsider the "old way" of thinking and recognize that if they hope to survive in the coming decades they will need to be all-inclusive in seeking out new perspectives from all sources of influence. These influences might include how global changes affect them and how they can effect global changes.

When we talk about Strategic Adaptability, we are talking about the reciprocation and impact of global changes on an organization. The diagram on page 59 provides a simple visual representation of the point we are trying to make. In the boxes labeled "Global Changes" we have given some examples to get you thinking about the types of global changes impacting your organization.

The Impact of Globalization

Globalization has fundamentally changed how organizations approach business. Our clients have felt the ramifications of global changes in the way they strategically adapt. This is one more reason that leaders must be flexible and open-minded in their thinking. To really "mine the gold" within an organization, Strategists should be prepared to receive responses that are different from what they expect and be willing to adapt their course of action to achieve the best results.

We have found many leaders looking at their organizations from the inside out (this is one level up from "navel gazing"). They get so focused on making and selling their products that they lose awareness of the needs and buying behaviors of their customers. Our counsel to these leaders is that you cannot be insular in a global era.

C2C Concept

A real-time example of Strategic Adaptability is "Cradle to Cradle Design," or the C2C approach. When leaders use the C2C approach they envision with a loop economy in mind. In a loop economy, the supply chain is utilization oriented or, more simply put, products and services are reused. This concept is different from the "linear economy," where the supply chain is production oriented and products usually have only one use. The C2C model is more holistic, economical, and ecologically focused because C2C is all about creating systems that are not just efficient, but that are also waste free. The C2C design was created by Walter R. Stahel in the 1970s. The current C2C model is based on a system of "lifecycle development" further developed by Michael Braungart.

To give a real-life example of C2C design, Boston architect William McDonough used this concept and began a new Industrial Revolution in how buildings are built. Buildings are constructed in which there are no sacrifices, just smart design that includes sustainability and clean technology. The concepts within "Cradle to Cradle" do not just reduce waste, they eliminate the *concept* of waste. We present this example because what Braungart and McDonough did was to strategically adapt their thinking from *linear* to *loop* thinking.

Strategic Adaptability has endless possibilities. In the 21st century, there is an enormous marketplace for ideas that work, and there will always be competitors out there who will adapt their strategies to make a profit. The Strategist achieves this reality and performs with excellence in this new age of visionary theorizing and adapting. The Strategist knows that if an organization is not able to strategically adapt, it will probably have its obituary in the *Wall Street Journal*, *Fortune* magazine, or *Forbes* magazine as one of the companies that did not make it.

Beyond Coping, Compromising, and Recalibrating

When we talk about being adaptable, we are not proposing taking a "dartboard" approach to strategic planning—a process of randomly throwing a dart at a list of options and wherever the dart lands that is the direction the leader takes. We are not even proposing that you consider strategic planning as one big *crisis d'jour* that must constantly be responded to. Agile Change Leadership goes beyond coping, compromising, and recalibrating. Today, plans must always be adaptable. The time has come to use a new kind of capability, one that unfortunately does not seem to exist today.

Agile leaders need to

– Conduct strategies in real time (not a three- to five-year plan).
– Be connected to shifts in the competitive environment (consider taking a different course with a different perspective).
– Completely understand and promote change and be aware of limitations and the need to expand on strengths.

When adapting, the Strategist makes functional switches and, at the same time, is flexible enough to get the right opportunities in place for success. This makes the central challenge for leaders and organizations to establish a sustainable balance within their environment and within the global economy. Leaders who act as a conduit between the environment, strategies of the organization, and procedures and structures within the organizational system will positively impact the profits of the organization. We promise!

Lessons from the Dakota Indians

There is an interesting tale about the principles of the Dakota Indians in the United States as it relates to the leader having both the wisdom to adapt and to change course in response to the new reality. The Dakota Indians are the largest division of the Siouan family. During the Revolution and the War of 1812, the Dakota Indians made peace with the United States and established boundary lines between the United States and various tribes in the northwest part of the country. The Dakota are universally considered to be superior—physically, mentally, and probably morally—to any of the western tribes. Their bravery has never been questioned by the "white man" or by the other Indian tribes as they conquered or drove out every rival except the Chippewa. Some well-known Dakota chiefs that you might have heard of are Sitting Bull, Crazy Horse, Red Cloud, and Crow King.

Dakota tribal wisdom stresses Strategic Adaptability and not the type of adaptability that continues on a course that clearly does not serve any purpose other than "we have always done it that way before." In *Leading the Revolution*, Gary Hamel points out Dakota tribal wisdom says that when you discover you are sitting on a "dead horse," the best step is to dismount and think differently about how you will complete your journey.

We have found organizations often try approaches that are familiar to them whether or not they add value to the solution. Executive leaders often keep the "dead horse" in the role in which it has always been and adapt the situation only as far as they feel comfortable. Hamel has made some recommendations on the most common approaches for dealing with a "dead horse" that include the following actions:

1. Buying a stronger whip.
2. Changing riders.
3. Saying, "This is the way we have always ridden this horse."
4. Appointing a committee to study the horse.
5. Arranging visits to other sites to see how *they* ride dead horses.
6. Increasing the standards for riding dead horses.
7. Appointing a task team to revive the dead horse.
8. Creating a training session to increase our riding ability.
9. Comparing the state of dead horses in today's environment.
10. Passing a resolution declaring, "This horse is not dead."
11. Blaming the horse's parents.
12. Harnessing several dead horses together for increased speed.
13. Declaring that "no horse is too dead to beat."
14. Providing additional funding to increase the horse's performance.
15. Doing a study to see if contractors can ride it cheaper.
16. Declaring the horse is "better, faster, and cheaper" dead.
17. Forming a quality circle to find uses for dead horses.
18. Revisiting the performance requirements for horses.
19. Promoting the dead horse to a supervisory position.

In respect to a "dead horse," it is time to dismount and accept the reality of the situation. When a strategic plan hits a bump in the road, is just not working, or throws the leader off course, the best response is to be agile, flexible, adaptable, and encouraging.

Strategic Adaptability Change Process

The stages of change below provide a way of thinking about change and changing strategy. It is intended to illustrate how a leader can move an organization through a development process and reach success. It also points out what a leader must do to help the organization progress from one level to the next during those often politically charged times of change. Once Strategists help the organization reach a new status quo, they are then poised to start the process again with as much agility and adaptability as when first beginning.

The promise of this model is that adapting and changing does occur and needs to occur for the organization to be relevant, valuable, and sustainable.

STATE OF BALANCE

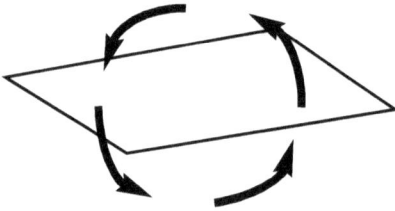

Key Word: Equilibrium

During This Phase: People are comfortable with the current situation and functionality. Everyone is aligned with the processes and systems within the organization.

Leadership Needed to Move to Next Level: Understand the organization's current strategy and objectives as well as how you can contribute to meet company objectives. Recognize that the future is shaped by present responses and any new strategy needs to link the organizational goals to the individual's motivation. This type of *linking* is a daily occurrence. The leader provides empathic listening and recognizes that people need a compelling reason to change. The leader also understands change dynamics and encourages people to seek improvement, information, and concepts from outside the group.

DEVELOPMENT

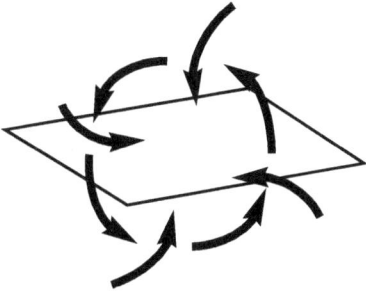

Key Word: Input

During This Phase: People are creating an awareness of the need for change and a willingness to take risks.

Leadership Needed to Move to Next Level: Leaders encourage the creation of new ideas, which challenge and encourage people to take risks and provide continuous engagement opportunities. Use triggers for creating new ideas and systems that capture innovation. Take responsibility by developing both a learning organization and formats for communication and consultation.

CHANGE

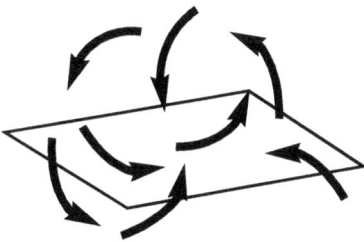

Key Word: Disorientation

During This Phase: People are scrambling to find successful patterns, develop better products, deliver external services, and uncover the most effective marketing strategy. It is a phase filled with excitement and energy, discovery and breakthrough. There is high energy and enthusiasm in this stage.

Leadership Needed to Move to Next Level: Listen to and understand responses from the market and employees. Provide high motivation and energy to people, maintain integrity, and provide increased levels of internal and external communication. Define the behavior you want and guide people to change by helping them learn new behaviors. Reward people when strategies are on track. In this phase, the leader helps people open up, become aware of the reasons for resistance, and overcome the common reactions to deny, avoid, or blame other people for the change.

CRISIS AND CONFLICT

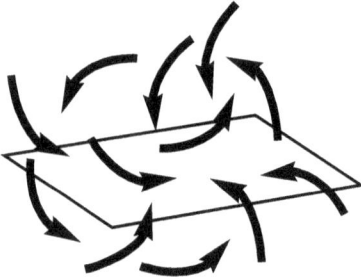

Key Word: Resistance

During This Phase: People protect their self-interests and narrow their views to survive the situation. In this phase they choose to avoid, defer, or confront.

Leadership Needed to Move to Next Level: Allow time for the "grieving process" as people stop using those techniques familiar to them. Help people relate the change to their inner world; help them internalize by enabling them to focus on their feelings, acknowledge their fears, and use support systems to move forward. In this phase, the leader helps build a safe environment that offers reassurance and helps find new methods for coping with difficulties, avoiding any attempt to short-circuit this stage with magical solutions, and honoring this stage as a natural process toward the overall goal.

NEW STATE OF BALANCE

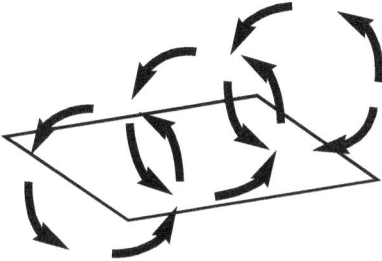

Key Word: Temporary Stability

During This Phase: Leaders continue to strategically adapt and change by providing new information that helps change behavior, attitudes, and values within the organization and its structure.

Leadership Needed to Move to Next Level: Help people reach a new status quo with support systems, resources, and reward mechanisms for maintaining the desired behavior. Build trust by providing clear communication of values and vision, continuing dialogue for future changes, and being open and congruent in your words and actions. By helping people feel safe and providing time to practice thinking and behaving in their new situation, the leader brings the organization to a new level.

The strategic adaptable process can be achieved in as quickly as one week or as long as six months, depending on the size and urgency of the project. As the rings of the new state of balance break off, the process begins again. We are always in a state of change, and the Strategist accepts and thrives on that understanding.

You might have noticed while reading through these stages that clear communication and over-communication are overriding themes that occur throughout the process. People will be more inclined to support change if they know what they are doing and why they are doing it. When those two questions are answered, the leader can begin to achieve "buy in" to the direction being taken and begin to continually adapt in achieving exceptional results.

The Strategic Adaptability Question

We want to emphasize that strategic planning is cyclical. Strategic Adaptability is a mindset that a Strategist takes toward accomplishing the plan.

Leaders with these abilities have few illusions of self-grandeur and are open to new opportunities. They recognize when the horse is dead and adapt to the situation. These leaders have the wisdom, courage, and determination to make tough decisions and to say "YES" or "NO" to establish a sustainable balance within their environment. A leader with these abilities can easily answer the question, "What prevents me from being more adaptable, and what can I do to develop a strong, agile mindset?"

STRATEGIST TRAIT

#3

▲ RESOURCES FOR INNOVATION ▼

Pretty much, Apple and Dell are the only ones in
this industry making money. Dell makes it by
being Wal-Mart. We make it by innovation.

STEVE JOBS
Co-founder, chairman, and CEO of Apple Inc.

Being innovative is making the quantum leap from "what has always been done" to "how can we do it better?" Innovative leaders are willing to open their minds and twist, divide, elaborate, conjure up, and develop thoughts to produce an innovative idea. They take initiative instead of waiting to be told what to do. They generate useful alternatives and thereby make decisions.

Being innovative means having the willingness and desire to explore, attempt, and achieve.

Disruptive Innovation

As an innovative Strategist, the ABL has the ability to deal with complexity, ambiguity, and uncertainty and can act decisively with incomplete information. That sounds like a big task, yet for the Strategist it is an everyday occurrence. The Strategist accepts situations as opportunities and is challenged to stretch in new directions and evoke higher levels of thinking. This type of leader has the ability to achieve results when others are stymied. This is because he or she uses all available Resources for Innovation, stretches beyond what seem to be reasonable limits, and redefines the boundaries of what seems constraining.

To be more clear, a problem solver tries to make something go away, whereas an innovator tries to bring something new into being. According to Steve Jobs, the innovative Strategist is labeled *"the crazy one, the misfit, the rebel, the troublemaker, the round peg in the square hole . . . he is the one who sees things differently and is not fond of rules. You can quote them, disagree with them, glorify or vilify them, but the only thing you can't do is ignore them because they change things . . . they push the human race forward, and while some may see them as the crazy ones, we see genius, because the ones who are crazy enough to think that they can change the world, are the ones who do"* (citing Jack Kerouac; quoted in an Apple Computer Ad, 1997, retrieved March 12, 2010, from http://lib.store.yahoo.net/lib/redlightrunner/thinkdifferent.mov). It is this type of disruptive innovation that inevitably leads to tremendous growth.

Changing the Context

This trait, Resources for Innovation, is all about strategically placing meaning and context onto things. For example, a paper clip can hold papers together in an office. In a laboratory, that same paperclip can act like a wire. For an individual, it could serve as a way to repair a pair of glasses. By changing the *context* of the item, you can create possibilities for your existing resources and form innovative solutions for skyrocketing forward. When Strategists dare to be innovative, they dare to *be* and *think* differently by stretching beyond what seems to be the reasonable limits, redefining the boundaries of what once could be considered and experienced as constraining.

This redefining and reformatting make innovation a strategic issue for a leader since innovation helps to

- ❍ Maintain a competitive edge.
- ❍ Improve productivity.
- ❍ Enhance financial performance.
- ❍ Improve communication.
- ❍ Promote learning.

Early in her career, Eileen worked in an insurance company. It did not take her long to realize that she would soon rot from the boredom and repetition in the organization. In addition to the dull duties of the job, all the deadpan faces of her colleagues sitting in their rows of desks and putting in time until the clock told them it was quitting time was more than she could handle. To spice things up she decided to be a little innovative and create a "happy minute." At precisely 3:00 p.m. every day, she would sit in her office chair and spin around in circles for one minute. "But we shouldn't do that," people on her team protested, even though they laughed and looked forward with anticipation to 3:00 p.m. each day. When she invited her co-workers to join her, they unanimously said, "But we might get fired." Each day Eileen invited everyone to join her and pointed out that it was a one-minute event and a break from the agony. "Would the company really fire you for taking one minute to re-energize yourself?" Eileen asked. Within a week a few people had joined her, and after that, the entire department spun around in their chairs for one minute and laughed each day. You could set your clock by this group. You knew when it was exactly 3:00 p.m. because the chairs would start spinning and everyone was laughing.

What does this have to do with innovation and being a Strategist? A great deal. By taking time (one minute) to change the context, change the mood, and change the activity, the activity opened the mind and created opportunities for thinking differently. From spinning in chairs for one minute, the group created other ways to work together and accomplish tasks. Soon people from other departments wanted to work in this department, and often, people would stay after work just to chat and enjoy each other's company. What Eileen was achieving by doing something different was affecting the culture and, in turn, effecting innovation. Or perhaps the other way around? It just depends on the context. In this case, Eileen saw humor as a central element of operational strategy and improving conditions at work. It was her small resource for innovation. She knew everyone needs to be able to laugh at themselves because we are not perfect. Laughing takes the edge off the seriousness of things and helps open the mind to let other possibilities pop in.

This story has a sequel. In 1997 Eileen's story was written up in *301 Ways to Have Fun at Work*, written by Dave Hemsath and Leslie Yerkes. When they heard the story they liked the concept so much they decided to include it in their book.

The Depths of Innovation

If you think back to the context of the organization as a yacht, there are different levels of innovative people who interact while the ship sails.

Observers: Some people are happy just where they are. All they want to do is seek stability. They are comfortable with their situation and do not want anything to change for fear of upsetting the status quo. Their experiences and education have brought them this far, and that is all they believe they need. Their innovative mind is in a resting state. They are happy to sit on the back of the yacht in a comfy seat and watch innovation happen.

Crew: These people can be counted on to do the job well. They have the skills and abilities to accomplish the task as requested. They do what is expected of them, no more and no less. Their innovative mind will only work within the confines of the job and the space. Innovation fits within defined boundaries.

Yacht designers: These people are perceived as "way out there," and others often feel they need reining in. They are filled with a wealth of new and bright ideas, yet they lack the experience and expertise to master the art of sailing. They are keen to do, try, experiment, and see what happens when they do something different or rock the proverbial boat. They can be high-pressured, intense, excessive, extreme, crazy, or irrational. They are anxious to be the first at creating a new way of sailing and have all the enthusiasm in the world to ride the waves. Their innovative minds are fresh, without the scars and bruises of previous voyages.

Skippers: These people are more like the ABL Strategist. They are ready for action and have the wisdom to keep matters in context and look out toward the vast sea of opportunity. They are skilled, capable, and equipped to face what is ahead. They have a positive attitude and a high level of confidence and courage. They are innovative and quickly create solutions to issues without becoming paralyzed by fear. Their minds are open, and experience has filled them with confidence and a desire to seek more.

As the Strategist leads the "organizational yacht," so to speak, she or he must be keenly aware of Resources for Innovation and how to harness them.

Creating an Innovative Culture

Culture represents the organization's conventional wisdom and is directly related to its purpose. Innovative cultures accentuate the success of the past, evoke images of possible futures, and create a spirit of restless, ongoing inquiry, taking people to new levels of activity and results. We consider culture as being one of the best Resources for Innovation for the ABL Strategist.

An organization's culture has two key components: business environment and values.

1. Business environment is affected by the marketplace. It is dependent on its products, competitors, customers, technologies, and government influences. The Breckenridge Institute found that trends and pace of the business environment have the single greatest influence in shaping an organization's culture.

2. Values are the basic concepts and beliefs of an organization. Values define "success" in concrete terms for employees. "If you do

this, you will be a success." They also establish the standards of achievement within the organization. Values provide a sense of common direction for all employees and guidelines for their day-to-day behavior. Values and culture matter only if they are lived and practiced every day.

An organization succeeds because its people can identify, embrace, and act on the values and environment of the organization.

Communication as an Innovation Resource

One organization with which we worked was having difficulty getting people to come "on board" within the organization. We helped their leadership send out a monthly message to stakeholders as part of their communication strategy to

- Explain what their collaborators and competitors were doing at the time.
- Share information on the trends they saw occurring in the industry.
- Inform everyone about what the organization was currently focused on.
- Ask the question, "What could we do differently to keep ahead of the rest?"

This type of communication helps everyone in the organization remain educated on current realities and face the existence of competition challenges. It also gives people the "current status quo" and encourages them to be open to innovating new possibilities. This is just one example of how communication can be considered an innovative resource for everyone involved in the organization. When a Strategist shares and personifies the organizational values and the type of environment expected, this opens up the channels for innovation to flourish.

Enabling Innovation

New and innovative possibilities for action are not only opportunities that can be used, they are also shocks that unsettle the existing culture and help to build a new and more agile culture. Agile Business Leaders know that promoting and embracing innovation distinguish them from traditional leaders and managers and understand that "today's mighty oak was once a small nut that held its ground in the backyard" of the organization at some time in the past!

Providing the Resources for Innovation to achieve fundamental changes for sustainable growth relies on six vital enablers.

1. Develop an innovative working environment
   - Where inspiration can thrive and continuous creativity can generate a flow of new ideas.
   - Where incubation structures and systems support the development and growth of new ideas to become innovations.

2. Promote collaboration and partnering
   - Work internally and externally with other organizations and specialists who have the strongest capabilities for innovation.
   - Integrate different perspectives, business insights, and technological capabilities into the environment to massage ideas and achieve innovation.

3. Display a willingness to be open
   - Hear, consider, and accept ideas from outside sources.
   - Recognize ideas and encourage the development of even more different alternatives.

4. Encourage controversy
   - Encourage people to say what they think and what solutions they have.
   - Know that if you always have "yes" people agreeing with you, either you or they are redundant.

5. Detect the dysfunctional
   - Immediately assess, remove, and learn from dysfunctional events.
   - Dysfunctions can stifle innovation, constrict thinking, remove mental stimulation, and destroy an organization's ability to compete.

6. Recognize talent
   • Honor the people who are willing to take risks.
   • Challenge the status quo and experiment to make things better.

The Resources for Innovation Question

The ability to synthesize obscure sources of information, research alternatives, and transform ideas into new concepts and methods requires Resources for Innovation. The six points above describe the behaviors of the Strategist in developing Resources for Innovation. A leader with these behaviors can easily answer the question, "How can I capture new and valuable solutions that will create a powerful positive impact on the organization?"

STRATEGIST TRAIT

#4

PATH TO MORE PROFITABILITY

Do not go where the path may lead.
Go instead where there is no path and leave a trail.
RALPH WALDO EMERSON
American essayist, philosopher, and poet

Strategists understand the correlation between employee engagement and business results. Their communication clearly articulates company strategies and objectives to people within the organization so the workforce is able to internalize and operationalize those objectives to deliver results. They get prepared to act quickly and put the best person on the project.

Planning for Profits

Many times we have heard people say about their leaders, "He is smart, and he knows the business, but his people skills are extremely poor, and he just doesn't know how to build business partnerships, so the business is suffering." This is why we stress that the ABL is *not* a Strategist, or a Specialist, or a Champion, or an Enabler. The ABL is a person with competencies in all of these areas. In these tumultuous times, it is not only critical to have a competitive edge, it is equally critical to be able to execute the plan, achieve results, and create profit. The difference between a useless strategic plan and a strong, well-executed one is (among other things) the ability to achieve sustainability and profitability.

In 1920, Alfred Sloan, an American automobile executive for General Motors, wrote a detailed analysis of what he believed were the failures of General Motors. In that analysis, he presented ways he thought General Motors should organize itself and avoid "ruin." He included an organizational chart and a specific plan for introducing financial controls, maximizing communications and efficiencies, and building profitability. He showed the report, titled "Organization Study," to the president, Pierre DuPont, and the CEO, Billy Durant. DuPont was very impressed. Durant never reacted to the report.

This now famous and regularly used document called the "Organizational Plan" that came out of Sloan's study is commonly copied by corporations, governmental agencies, and nonprofit organizations eager to create a sustainable business direction. Organizational plans used today typically identify the key targets, revenues, operating margin, cash flow, productivity, market share, and capital expenditure of an organization. Unfortunately, for all the good organizational plans do, they can often drain energy from the organization by diverting its management into useless game playing. For example, a rigid budget can cause a leader to miss opportunities over the course of the year. A budget in an organizational business plan may drive the strategic plan and can force people to make poor decisions when they are desperate to reach their targets. You might hear people say . . .

"Let's spend it now, whether we need the thing or not, just to make sure we get the same amount next year."

"Let's make sure we load inventory into the pipeline just before the end of the quarter to pump up the numbers."

"Let's fudge the description so we can use the money in this account instead of this other one."

You probably have heard other comments with the same tone.

Riding the Waves to Profit

The management theorist, Peter Vaill, wrote a book titled *Strategies for Survival in a World of Permanent Whitewater*. When we hear the term "whitewater," most people think about the turbulent flow of water over a riverbed. Whitewater foams and creates currents and whirlpools and causes great disruption to the river and to anyone floating on it. Vaill considers "permanent whitewater" in the world of leadership and organizations as a concept of experiencing accelerated change, growing uncertainty, and increasingly unpredictable global connections of economics, technology, and people. The "permanent whitewater" effect produces irreversible and unfocused change, requiring organizations to alter their course or face serious disruption.

If one continues to think of the organization as a yacht (with the purpose of creating a path to increased profitability), then the leader must ride the turbulent waves and maintain an organizational plan that invents unprecedented forms of data collecting, solution building, and agile approaches to building profitability. Eileen's son is a whitewater river guide. He says, "When I am navigating a Class 5 river [the ones that require advanced whitewater experience because of the large waves, rocks, and dangers], I am always aware of the risks, but more important, I must be ready to think fast, react quickly, and be prepared for the unknown and the unforeseen. There is nothing static, fixed, or constant about riding in a boat on a whitewater river. But when we succeed, it's a great rush and sense of accomplishment because we responded, adjusted, and guided the boat and the riders through troubled waters."

For this trait, we emphasize that the future of profitability does not just happen through a well-crafted organizational plan; leaders cannot delude themselves by thinking the plan will work from start to finish without a problem. Leaders must exercise all the discipline, imagination, and agility they can muster to deal with the ever-present unanticipated events and create a path to increased profitability.

Profits and the Future

Translating plans, no matter how well-crafted, into profitability depends on how well the leader leverages the human capital within the organization. For example:

> IN THE LATE 1970s, Alvin Toffler, an American writer and futurist, known for his work in the digital communications revolution, attended a dinner party held for the then Chinese ambassador. Toffler found himself seated with the top executives from the National Broadcasting Company (NBC) and the Radio Corporation of America (RCA). Toffler took advantage of this opportunity to ask them how broadcasting would be different economically in five years. Both men smiled slowly and assured Toffler there would be no major changes. They, like other leaders, would lose their jobs in the years ahead for not seeing the approaching changes and incremental adjustments which needed to be made in order to survive. You could say they were asleep at the helm and proud of it. Toffler, who wrote *Future Shock* in 1971, saw the knowledge age as an outgrowth of the industrial age that would require only a bit of fine tuning. Today reality has taken even Toffler by surprise, who now sees the knowledge age as more revolutionary than anticipated. What remains is still frothing and changing its shape. It is a whole new era, with dangers and opportunities uniquely its own. (Retrieved January 10, 2009, from http://www.skypoint.com/members/mfinley/toffler.htm)

Moving toward profitability requires a realization that whitewater is a reality, and we must plan for it. In the past, leaders could choose one of three ways to bring the organization into a state of profitability. They could be

1. Reactive: Waiting for an opportunity to present itself and then pouncing on the opportunity. In essence, these leaders were acting through default. A reactive strategy is designed to keep options open and provide the necessary flexibility to cope with a wide range of occurrences.

2. Anticipative: Instead of waiting for an opportunity, developing procedures and strategies within the organization to anticipate ways to become more profitable. Preplanning is achieved by developing new cultures and competencies in anticipation of more competitive conditions in the future.
3. Trailblazing: Creating new marketing niches and desires for products or services through innovation, marketing, lobbying, and collaboration with other organizations.

To thrive in today's business world, leaders must incorporate all these approaches, because each concept has its own value. It is not enough to know how the latest technology works. It is not enough to know what makes people tick and then react. It is not enough to anticipate sales, manufacturing, and cost accounting. It is not enough to always cut a new trail.

To make an organization accelerate toward being more profitable, a leader must get feedback from customers, suppliers, regulators, and local communities, those who have the potential to receive value from the organization's services and products. A leader must know the context of the here and now and respond to the emergence of the situation. Strategists make sure those within the organization (including themselves) really understand their customers, their customers' needs and buying behaviors, and the reasons for asking for changes in these behaviors. Understanding an organization's customers is one of the basics of business success. It is the real core to building profitability. Getting customers involved in helping provide them with the service they want is critical to building a strong business.

Taking Risks for Profitability

The confidence to take personal or business risks and to allow an opportunity to succeed is what drives Strategists toward profitability. Strategists are the chance takers; they travel on a different path and ride the whitewater to the unknown instead of safely heading down the old straight and narrow stream. They define the benchmark for quality and create an environment where excellence is expected. This skill includes the ability to create a shift in perception and practice.

Steve Jobs, CEO of Apple, suggests one approach for creating a Path to More Profitability. He says, "A lot of companies have chosen to downsize, and maybe that was the right thing for them. We chose a different path. Our belief was that if we kept putting great products in front of customers, they would continue to open their wallets" (retrieved June 3, 2010, from MacObserver, August 13, 2003, an article entitled "Steve Jobs on Optimism, Innovation, Apple, Profitability, Piracy, and More," http://www.macobserver.com/article/2003/08/13.6.shtml). This approach transforms thinking from an administrative goal-setting process to an Agile Business Leader approach, including getting the business lines to take ownership for the quality and delivery, resulting in performance and profitability. This type of agile thinking leads to quality, usability, efficiency, and exceptional delivery.

The challenge for leaders wanting to build a Path to More Profitability lies not in choosing the right organizational plan; it lies in an ability to integrate small details with the grand themes. An example of this might be the Burj located in Dubai. The Burj is the world's tallest tower and the centerpiece of the Gulf region's most prestigious urban development to date. The Burj is so tall that lightning will strike its side, not its spire. Some of the elevators, operating under auxiliary power, can serve as lifeboats if the need arises. One of the small details in building this enormous structure was strategizing how to pump concrete into the sky and keep it from cracking in the blazing sun. The answer was to mix it at night with ice (retrieved March 13, 2010, from http://www.moreintelligentlife.com/story/tallest-building-world).

When we talk about strategizing in this chapter, we are talking about a leader understanding what kind of permanent and non-permanent whitewater must be maneuvered through when riding the wave to achievement. When a leader looks at the wrong details and draws the wrong conclusions, chances are he or she will create the wrong path to profitability and, in some cases, drown.

It is one of the Strategist's roles to assess if the organization has the right structures, resources, information, and people to create a profit. It is also the Strategist's role to see, test, and probe the situation for potential opportunities to create profitability.

The Path to Profitability Question

What makes a leader foolish or wise, understanding or blind, knowledgeable or inept is how the leader perceives each situation and assesses specific differences. The description of this trait and its competencies explains the Path to More Profitability. The Strategist knows that spending time trying to develop the perfect organizational plan will be in vain because reality will dictate a different path at some stage of implementation. A leader with these abilities can easily answer the question, "Where will future profits come from and how can we capture them?"

CONCLUSION TO STRATEGIST

As consultants, we have noticed a lot of organizations negating the concept of "business strategy" and replacing it with the phrase "business model." Organizations use this concept as a way of thinking that business success is less about the logistics of the strategy and more about the quality of its products or the innovativeness of its people. The Strategist thinks about the value of the anchor on the sailboat, as well as the strength of the sails and the capability of the crew. The Strategist knows that sometimes you have to stop and take stock of the current conditions and sometimes you have to venture out to the far and endless sea.

Organizational concepts abound in leadership seminars where people hear all the right noises about strategy, dealing with resistance to change, and understanding why employee participation is more likely to build commitment. What leaders do not always learn are the best approaches for shifting attitudes and linking the strategy to action or about designing to new levels of quality output and satisfaction by the end user.

Creating an organization with a compelling environment and clearly articulated goals takes thought and effective strategies. The words and jargon used for steering an organization through "permanent whitewater" might distort the way we think about strategizing business. Yet at the same time, leaders know all too well that increased competition as a result of globalization, along with the rise of the knowledge economy, has caused changes in how leaders strategize and plan. Many of the repercussions of changing leadership expectations and economic developments over the coming decades will accelerate changes in what is expected from strategic business leaders.

Hyper-competition, connectivity, and breakthrough technologies are mandating changes at a faster rate than ever before. If leaders continue using their old ways of operating, they will probably still have a hard time implementing strategies that are supposed to help people adapt and prosper.

Bright Idea

At this point, we are reminded of the story of the king during the Dark Ages who wanted more light in his castle. He challenged the people to create new candles that would burn hotter and brighter. He called for a new strategy for increasing light in the castle. The townspeople created all sorts of options and brought all types of new candles to the king for his review. Some candles used new kinds of wicks and some used different kinds of wax for burning efficiency. None of the candles changed the lighting condition in the castle. In the end, one man (you could call him an Agile Business Leader) brought in ten candles to sell to the king. The candles were exactly the same as the original candles the king was using. (Stay with us, this townsperson/Agile Business Leader wasn't as crazy as you might think.)

The townsperson put the candles on the wall and made one significant strategic difference to how the candle was used. Behind each candle he placed a piece of glass. Each piece of glass had silver on one side to form a mirror. When the candles were lit, the light reflecting against the glass lit up as it had never done before. Needless to say, the man won the contest and the contract for producing more candles and candle holders for the king. The moral of this Strategist story: it doesn't matter how much quality you have; you have to know how to best use the energy and resources that you have to create brilliant results.

We encourage leaders to take a new line of strategic reasoning to align people strategies with business strategies to deliver further value and drive increased business performance. Sometimes those ideas can be as simple as adding a backdrop to the existing strategy. Sometimes those strategies produce more radical thinking. Strategists can move from the incremental to the radical, toward a fundamental revolution in their approach to productivity. We encourage leaders to bring out the best in people's innovation and use their ability to anticipate and infer the future to support the change toward that future.

What separates Strategists from robots, androids, and microprocessors is the ability to think strategically and improvise as reality continues around them. Each time reality throws Strategists an unplanned situation, they do not panic and instantly reach for a lifeboat. Instead, they stay committed to the current situation with laser beam focus and flashes of innovation to create a solution and a better future.

The desire to drive change and deliver results is key in transporting people to an entirely different place from structures and predictable sustainability to formlessness and uncertainty. Today's strategic planning calls for a new way of thinking about business and about capitalizing on resources.

Push Back the River

Nobody is skilled enough to "push back the river." These days, most things do not hold still long enough to be both diagnosed and changed in an incremental way. No leader can know all the ins and outs of any system and take time to isolate, analyze, and synthesize it into many parts. What we suggest is for leaders to be skilled enough to create opportunities for their people to feel they are part of the solution and hence become the architects of their own success.

This makes the Strategist one who conceptualizes, a person who understands the organization and shapes the way it works. A Strategist knows that success hinges on the ability to understand and anticipate the way business infrastructures change and the ability to leverage resources.

The competencies of the Strategist are driven by

- Staying ahead of new realities.
- Understanding how people best receive information.
- Understanding how people trade knowledge.

- Learning how to best shape perceptions.
- Forming strong relationships.
- Creating visions of the future that evoke confidence.

Steve Jobs was once heard saying to an employee,

YOUR TIME IS LIMITED, so don't waste it living someone else's life. Don't be trapped by dogma—which is living with the results of other people's thinking. Don't let the noise of other's opinions drown out your own inner voice and most important, have the courage to follow your heart and intuition. You somehow already know what you truly want to become. Everything else is secondary.

(Commencement address by Steve Jobs, CEO of Apple Computer and of Pixar Animation Studios, delivered on June 12, 2005, to Stanford University)

The Strategist knows the answer to the question, "Do you want your skills and abilities to be anchors or sails in an unforgettable adventure?" The choice is yours; it always has been.

Eileen was born in Winnipeg, Manitoba, Canada, which is officially labeled as the coldest city in the world. The combination of very low temperatures and high wind speed is dangerous—and can be life threatening. Weather forecasters in Manitoba issue warnings not to venture out in such conditions particularly when temperatures can dip to −45° C with a wind chill factor of −57° C (these numbers are NOT exaggerated!). Winnipeg winter is a time of hardship, survival, and extremes, along with great and unexpected beauty. Living in such a city provides an opportunity to use your ingenuity in the face of nature's might (as long as you don't expose your hands or other extremities for too long!). It is an opportunity to set systems in place to handle the infrastructure required to survive. This mentality has a lot of similarities to the role of the Strategist.

No matter what opportunities are presented to a leader, the Strategist believes in the power of hard work, the malleability of thinking, and intelligent questioning. The collective intelligence available to everyone has not shrunk; it has merely evolved. People have become quicker, broader-minded, and more self-aware. For this reason, the Strategist knows success is based *less* on professional expertise and *more* on considering a variety of expanded options, a good dose of common sense, and being agile in everything he or she does.

Ideas in Action

Developing complex strategy is often the easiest part of creating a new world. In the Middle East, the phrase "strategic development" is used more often than words like "oil" and "gas," and water is more expensive than fuel. Leaders across the Middle East have been busy creating tourist magnets and a sort of "sand groper's guide" to the rich and famous. It seems that every day someone there is touting that they are building the tallest structure in the world or the biggest man-made island or a ski resort in a shopping center. Turning such grandiose strategies into reality requires an ability to deploy that strategy with clarity and simplicity. The most successful corporate strategies are the ones where everybody in the organization is informed and is given the opportunity to support and implement the strategy.

Qatar, to the north of Dubai and a one-time laggard in the battle of one-up-man-ship that has been raging among the wealthy sheiks, decided in 2007 to create its first off-shore island resort, to be named "The Pearl."

The concept of a city built on a man-made island, which had all its services managed by an invisible team of "condo cleaners" and facilitators, was not understood in this part of the world. We were asked to help with educating the community on exactly what a "managed facility" was and how it operated. In *Nexus* magazine, the following Cartaphor was used to educate the community on the mega-project called "The Pearl Qatar." When this project is completed in 2011, it will house enough people to increase the country's population by 6 percent—that is about forty thousand people in one complex, well city, really. The editor's message stated, "Complementing our cover story, the cover image

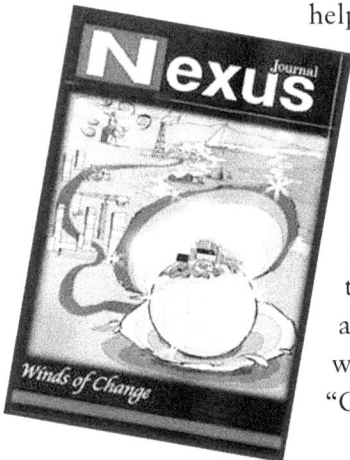

is a Cartaphor, a combination of a metaphor and a cartoon. It depicts the connection to the shamal (northern wind), which creates change by shaping the desert. The sand grain carried by the wind fertilizes the oyster that eventually gives birth to a pearl. The image depicts the winding road from the discovery of oil and gas, to the construction of commercial and residential properties, supported by public infrastructure and the creation of spectacular and visionary mega projects such as The Pearl-Qatar."

The leaders of this project recognized the value of the Cartaphor for deploying their strategy across the Middle East community. The Cartaphor was cleverly used by the editorial staff at *Nexus*, where they extracted specific elements of the Cartaphor to assist with the visualization of different pieces of the puzzle.

QUESTIONS TO CONSIDER

These questions are designed to increase awareness and challenge some of your current thinking. They are designed to help you develop a more agile mindset and can be used to help explain your vision and what it means to you and everybody in the organization.

Imagine yourself using this Cartaphor to refine a strategy for your organization. Answer the following questions:

1. What new products, services, or alliances could emerge as a "pearl" in your organization?
2. What conscious and unconscious reactions do you need to be prepared for as you serve a multitude of customers?
3. What people, systems, structures, or functionalities need to be added for the organization to alter the competitive landscape?
4. How well will your customers respond to the quality of your product or service?
5. How can you use the proverbial "shamal" (northern wind) to change the environment of the organization and meet industry demands and support the changing needs of customers?

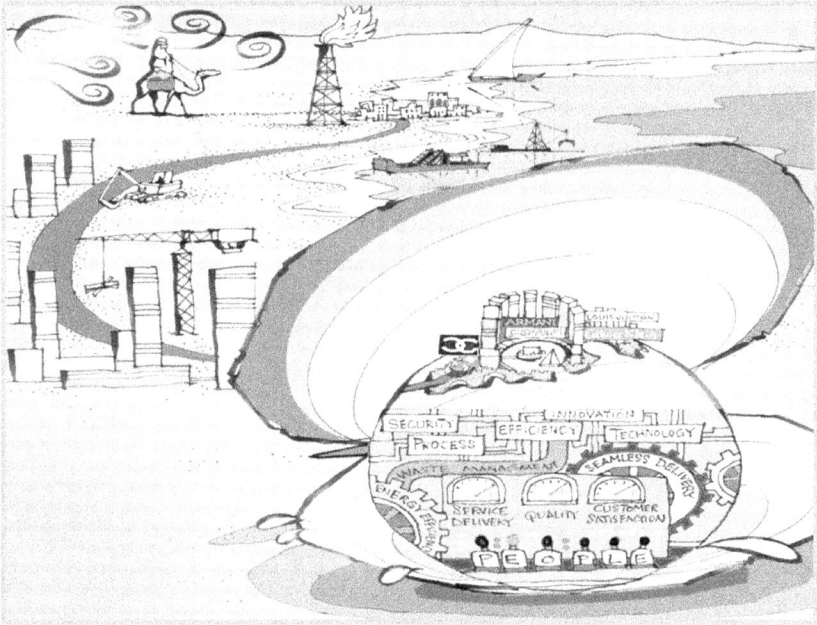

6. What milestones need to be created to execute the plan and bring it to fruition?
7. How will the ebbs and flow of the tides impact your organizational direction?
8. How will the possibility of a hundred-year flood impact your strategy?
9. What competitors will come by land or by sea?
10. What is your personal "pearl" for the future?

PERSONAL ACTION PLAN

Self-assessment and adaptability are extremely important as an Agile Business Leader. We suggest you devise a personal plan to accomplish changes you want to implement for yourself or for your organization. Ask the question, "What actions or changes in my behavior do I need to accomplish and by when?" Then construct an Action Plan that will help you achieve your goal. Write it down and monitor it or use your community of practice to help you become even more accountable for your actions.

Action Plan

	Action Item	Resources Required	Date of Completion
1			
2			
3			
4			

What actions or changes in my behavior do I need to accomplish? How soon?

_____

_____

_____

3

THE ENABLER

❖ *Facilitates Action* ❖

Action speaks louder than words but not nearly as often.

MARK TWAIN
American author and humorist

I n the role of Enabler a leader responds to the two realities of needing to be people-focused and at the same time needing to achieve
action. The Enabler is focused on helping the group dynamics of the organization by working to optimize talent and leverage the strengths of
all generations to work and mobilize results. The Enabler transforms
his or her talents to make things happen. Enablers are the activists of
the organization.

The four traits of the Enabler are

❐ Outcomes
❐ Motivation
❐ Learning in Action
❐ Collaborative Cultures

In the role of Enabler a leader inspires and motivates for outstanding
performance. Enablers are resilient to breaks in communication channels because they have strong collaboration skills and continually search
for ways of engaging the masses and building organizations that continually learn, adapt, evolve, and improve. They do not become en-
meshed in the petty details or emotional dramas that can distract their
focus from where it belongs. Instead, Enablers have the innate ability to
impart a sense of invincibility, power, and control over the situation.
They are incredibly driven, which in turn rubs off on their followers.
They tap into reserves of the minds, hearts, and souls of people and
know which "buttons" to push to activate, faith, hope, drive, and perseverance. The Enablers do not put their focus on authority. They are
more about influence, loyalty, and building trust. They communicate an
optimistic, bright, enticing picture of the future and share information
for cultivating and sustaining a preferred corporate culture. The Enablers are leaders who convince people to get on board and stay on
board. They make people feel good about them and make others feel
good about what they are accomplishing and achieving what they set
out to do.

LEADERS WHO MAKE A DIFFERENCE

Leadership is a complex concept defined as the ability to influence, motivate, and enable others to contribute to the effectiveness and success of the organization. Whatever definition you use to define leadership, the basic assumption about leadership is that leaders "make a difference." They align organizational goals with people needs to bring success to the organization. Leaders align people and organizational goals.

All four areas of the Agile Business Leader model are needed to turn disaffected and disengaged employees into highly engaged go-getters.

PURPOSE OF THIS CHAPTER

In this chapter, we combine the competencies of the Enabler with a practical, "how-to" format that challenges leaders to use what they learn. Some of the tools and concepts we present will engage both the creative and practical approaches of Enabler leadership techniques. Some of the techniques will include

- Developing long-term perspectives.
- Blocking distractions.
- Seeking candid feedback.
- Stretching development.
- Reflecting on ways to improve and celebrate success.

Our intention with this chapter is to present information, ideas, and strategies to leaders for building a dynamic culture that engages employees at all levels of the organization and help leaders release the true potential of the people and the organization.

THE NEED FOR ENABLERS

For a very long time we have heard from the people we work with, as well as from our colleagues, that leadership is driven by the efforts of exceptional people with innate gifts, strategic insights, and limitless charisma. We have heard some leaders, with the best intentions, attempting to motivate their people toward an outcome, generate enthusiasm, and build momentum using incongruent words or actions. They kill an initiative on the spot. Highly effective leaders use their ability to inspire, influence, and develop others and, at the same time, ensure satisfaction for all stakeholders. This is the key component to leadership. A leader's ability to enable others to act with outstanding performance is critical to achieving business success.

ENABLING FOR ALIGNMENT

Enablers build better, stronger, and more authentic relationships. The competencies of the Enabler are focused on developing shared goals and integrative solutions, while at the same time building relationships based on trust. Leaders who are strong in the ABL Enabler role are often described as facilitative leaders. They are highly consultative and participatory in their leadership approach and help people to

- Challenge their assumptions.
- Explore alternatives.
- Develop shared goals.
- Promote accountability.
- Set standards for excellence.
- Foster competence.

THE ENGAGED AND DISENGAGED

In simple terms, there are two kinds of workers, the engaged and the disengaged. Engaged workers are the ones who are dedicated to the organization. They want to contribute and be truly productive. They are inspired by their work. Engaged workers care about the future of the organization and make an effort to exceed and help the organization succeed.

The disengaged workers are the ones who watch the clock and wait for quitting time. They do not know or understand the direction of the organization and show up to do the minimum amount of work possible. The disengaged employee is the one who is miserable and argumentative and who resists putting any effort into an initiative. To positively impact the engaged or disengaged worker, an Enabling leader is needed to fight the malaise and create a culture of optimism and engagement.

How well leaders use a two-way communication process will absolutely determine how well the organization will function and how well employees will gladly be engaged. If conversations are artificial, politicized, or fragmented, failure is more likely. If conversations are candid, open for debate, reality-based, and poised to search for realistic solutions, then success is imminent.

Many leaders have strength in at least one of four areas of the Agile Business Leader model (Specialist, Strategist, Champion, and Enabler). Truly great leaders have strengths in all four areas. The Agile Business Leader has the following characteristics:

- The proven knowledge and skills of the Specialist necessary for a leader to be a highly successful performer.
- The will, self-determination, motivation, and ethical character of the Champion combined with the stamina and courage to lead.
- The ability of the Strategist to respond to the current needs of the organization and build a more profitable future to lead the organization in sustainability and growth.
- The ability to deal within a global environment and the interpersonal skills of an Enabler to build learning initiatives and effectively deal with people to create a high-performing workforce.
- Enablers leverage the knowledge, wisdom, and resources of the organization's human capital so they can make faster decisions, share resources, collaborate, and build competence within the organization.

ENABLER TRAITS AND COMPETENCIES

Enablers amalgamate four traits with eight competencies to leverage the true sources of productivity and success. They understand the needs and capacities of other people around them, whether they are customers, suppliers, colleagues, supervisors, or staff. These eight Enabler competencies along with the competencies of the Champion, Strategist, and Specialist include the following:

Outcomes:
1. Develop collaborative processes for delivering outcomes.
2. Value and build upon group diversity.

Motivation:
3. Motivate people toward action.
4. Coach and mentor teams and individuals.

Learning in Action:
5. Develop learning environments.
6. Create productive working environments.

Collaborative Cultures:
7. Build relationships of trust.
8. Foster communication.

ENABLER TRAIT

#1

▲ OUTCOMES ▼

It is our attitude at the beginning of a difficult undertaking which, more than anything else, will determine its successful outcome.

WILLIAM JAMES
American Psychologist and Philosopher

Leaders traditionally have developed the capacity to analyze situations and solve problems in a logical, rational way. They take notice of what went wrong, search for causes, and propose alternate solutions. Their thinking is sound and mechanistic. The effectiveness of how leaders transfer their thinking to the creation of achievable results is reliant on the effectiveness of the messages they are sending to their team.

Allow us to give you an example borrowed from an experiment conducted in 1972 by two scientists named John D. Bransford and Marcia K. Johnson. The experiment involved presenting people with a description of a task to complete to achieve a specific outcome. We give the same instructions to you (the reader) and ask you to say in simple terms what task you are being asked to achieve.

The instructions are as follows:

Instructions to Achieve the Outcome

THE PROCEDURE IS ACTUALLY QUITE SIMPLE. First you arrange items into different groups. Of course one pile may be sufficient depending on how much there is to do. If you have to go somewhere else due to lack of facilities that is the next step; otherwise you are pretty well set. It is important not to overdo things. That is, it is better to do too few things at once than to do too many. In the short run this may not seem important but complications can easily arise. A mistake can be expensive as well. At first, the whole procedure will seem complicated. Soon, however, it will become just another facet of life. It is difficult to foresee any end to the necessity for this task in the immediate future, but then, one can never tell. After the procedure is completed one arranges the materials into different groups again. Then they can be put into their appropriate places. Eventually they will be used once more and the whole cycle will then have to be repeated. However, that is part of life.

Without knowing in advance the title or the topic of the task, the participants had a tough time completing and achieving the desired outcome based on reading the paragraph above. At this point, you as a reader might be just as confused at what the task actually is. If we told you before reading the instructions above that the task was "how to wash clothes," you might have comprehended the information much better and even recalled some information you already knew from your previous experiences of washing clothes. What is also interesting is that learning how to "wash clothes," based on these instructions, probably does not help you remember how to complete the task based on the procedure above. Basically our instructions were not as helpful as they could have been to get the achieved outcome.

We share this experience with you to emphasize that in order for an idea to come to fruition, people must be made aware of the topic or at least the actions must be put into context before they can begin selecting details for learning and retrieving past experiences. The challenge for the Enabler is to engage people through relevant and useful information and techniques so goals can be met and Outcomes can be achieved.

Wing Walkers

After World War I, there were a group of entertainers called Wing Walkers. As part of their routine they used a biplane (the type with an open cockpit). They would step onto the wing while the plane was in flight. The first rule of Wing Walking is "never let go of something until you're hanging on to something else." This advice seems to make good sense to the average person, especially while you are flying through the air with the wind in your face and the wing of the plane below your feet. A Wing Walker always reached out and put one hand on something of substance while continuing to cling to the new point of contact. As entertainers, Wing Walkers built a reputation of responsiveness and positive collaboration to achieve their outcome. They gave exceptional performances and attracted customers to see the show.

In a way, the Agile Business Leader is like a Wing Walker. With the complexity of choices in this current business climate, ABLs must step out "on their wing" with duality of thinking. On the one hand, they must reach for new opportunities to hold on to and get where they desire to go. On the other hand, they must draw strength and support from what they are currently clinging to.

When we work with leaders from around the world, they recognize the need for the following abilities:

- Working with their people to ensure operational plans travel along a predetermined course.
- Implementing performance measures that are aligned with the desired Outcomes.
- Giving feedback to employees that is aimed at developing the individual.
- Creating an organization or team that thrives on learning.

We encourage our clients to transform and advance their way of thinking about leadership to accelerate their organizational success. We encourage them to step out onto the "wing" and value the strengths of the existing system. When you use this form of thinking, or more specifically of the Agile Business Leader methodology, the leader takes a more adaptive approach to human capital management practices and the organization begins to yield positive results because the leader personifies these actions:

- Recognizes and values employees as individuals.
- Responds effectively to employees' needs.
- Understands the best approach for increasing employee motivation, commitment, and performance.

Global Standards of Excellence

We want to stress again that Enablers create standards of excellence and set examples for others to follow. They model the desired direction through personal example and are dedicated to the execution and practice of useful guidelines and pragmatic principles. To understand this concept from a real-world perspective, we talked to Patrick Carmichael from the Saudi Arabian Oil Company, Saudi Aramco. Saudi Aramco ranks number one among oil companies worldwide in terms of crude oil and natural gas production exports. It also operates an extensive network of refining and distribution facilities (Retrieved October 20, 2008, from http://www.jobsataramco.com/Home/Default.aspx).

In 2008 Patrick was inducted into the Best Practice Institute as a senior executive member. The Best Practice Institute describes itself as follows: "Best Practice Institute (BPI) is a community of leaders dedicated to pioneering and sharing best practices. BPI produces online learning sessions, Webinars, BPI work-groups™, on-site 'by invitation-only' thought leader and executive case driven conferences, research publications and a knowledge and certification portal for its subscribers. This group shares and pioneers innovative, emerging practices through best practice sharing sessions, site visits and customized research reports."

We have been working with Patrick, in conjunction with the International Institute for Facilitation, to assist in developing a facilitative leadership process for Saudi Aramco. By facilitative leadership, we mean a process where the company teaches and certifies employees as internal facilitators.

In his role at Saudi Aramco, Patrick specializes in identifying talent to meet the future needs of the organization and building executive leaders. As a person who works internationally, Patrick has a passion for learning and incorporating best practices into his organization. We asked Patrick for his views on what leadership capabilities are needed for building outstanding organizations.

IT IS ABOUT WHO YOU ARE AND WHAT YOU DO. It is about how you use the internal and external components of business to guide your actions.

External Component: From an external perspective, successful leaders model good leadership behavior. What they do and what others see they do is primarily important. Externally, leaders provide direction, they champion their people toward results, and they support their people in all ways possible. They provide decisions and make hard choices.

Internal Component: From an internal perspective, what you are as a leader is directly related to your core values. It's about how you use your values and your individual character to perform as a leader. Internally, leaders have a character that is open to learning, open to feedback, self-driven, and self-starting. These are natural characteristics for them. They have the knowledge, ability, and skills to communicate well. Good leaders constantly ask themselves who needs to know a particular piece of information and who needs to be informed. Their mind incorporates all aspects for consideration. They never blurt out their thoughts. Instead, they are more thoughtful about what they say because they recognize the power of the well-communicated message that flows outward.

One of my successful moments as a leader is not really about me individually, rather it is about how a team I led pulled together and accomplished their task. One of our tasks was to strengthen the ties between our offices in Houston, Texas, and Saudi Arabia. We built a strong relationship with the audit team and targeted a number of programs to build stronger ties with Saudi Arabia and form relationships with many individual stakeholders to help understand their issues. This task quadrupled the amount of work we did internally. It also caused us to pay attention to specifics of the business. Our attitude changed from human resource police to service providers.

We tied our work to the direction of the company, to the direction of the business. and to the business at hand. I worked with several ad hoc groups and helped them turn ideas into action and work the "white space." I was able to get people to develop and utilize their influence without positional power. It was a great project and the people whom we were serving felt more commitment to the company when it was completed.

Thinking back on this task, if I had to do it over again, I would have been more mindful of the dynamics of the team and paid more attention to the people we brought on board. I learned that even though we achieved success together, group dynamics can dent the performance of the team and thereby limit growth.

The way leaders communicate is also an important factor for success. Being able to dialogue and create consensus is a big part of success. Some leaders are constantly communicating to the point that everyone is confused. Communication should help people understand the message that leaders are trying to send. This means leaders needs to be open to feedback in terms of how they can improve their communication. When leaders communicate they need to keep three things in mind. These points need to become the core of leadership and values:

    i) Truth—who needs to know the information

    ii) Integrity—who needs to convey the information

    iii) Conviction—how best to explain the information so others understand it fully

Not only are these points critical in terms of what leaders value, but as a second step, they can also be acted upon.

Truth: Is a core-value. Truth includes seeking to know the truth about the business and oneself. When a leader is telling the truth, diplomacy is needed. It is also important to remember that your personal opinion might be misleading and can blur the truth. Having a willingness to seek out feedback is therefore critical in forming your initial thoughts on what is true. This means leaders must seek out truthful feedback on both a personal and a business level, no matter how uncomfortable it may become.

Integrity: Is the blending of honesty, fairness, ethics, and passion for doing what's right. It is about forthrightness. The leader with integrity does not ask others to do that which is not right. Ethics and truth cannot become blurred and must constantly be monitored. Successful leaders surround themselves with people who have integrity and are solid to the core and they do not include individuals who will pat them on the back in the hope that it will make them look good.

Conviction: Is the willingness to act on the truth. It is the leader's faithful pursuit right to the end. Conviction is persistence and resolve to do "what I say will be done, and it will be done till the end." It is more about being the workhorse that is willing to do the mission-critical work than the show horse that simply looks good.

Leaders are challenged today by a war on talent—the search for the best and the brightest becoming a constant costly battle—and a need to be open about moving into new growth areas. I am proud to say that Saudi Aramco is the world's largest oil company. We are the number-one company in the world and have enjoyed that success for seventy-five years. Now we must ask ourselves the question, "How do we continue to succeed?" We know we need to draw new borders and bring new ideas to the table.

For the longest time all we did was produce. Now we have to move into fuller integration, move faster, and look at different business models. We have a culture that is risk adverse. We see the importance in leaders being agile. We see the need for a different generation of leaders to take over power in the organization. We have successfully re-engineered our risk adversity and now we do more innovative work.

We have gone from a "focus on production" and evolved into a fully integrated energy company. We are in transition and with transition come the challenges and opportunities. With all that is going on in the world we must be willing to be agile in our current thinking to transform ourselves and be more responsible to a successful future.

With the need for agile thinking and building a company of leaders, we know that one of our challenges will be to challenge traditions. Behavior based on tradition is a very strong component in this part of the world. With tradition come values. It is these strong family and country values that we must carefully consider and work with while moving the company forward. As a leader, I know that a person, country, or even organization's values can "hold you in" and make you unwilling to do something new and different. At the same time, values can present opportunities to embrace and be used as springboards to the next step. For example, some might think that we are only an oil company. This is not true for we are also in the business of infrastructure development because we consider the employee as a whole person, a person with values. When we make changes we consider changes to the whole person and the culture they live in. Along with being an oil company we also build roads, schools, and hospitals, and recently we even built a university. We do this because when we are called upon to help, we do. We do because we value the whole system as part of our work.

In my part of the world (Saudi Arabia) we value age. Age is one of my biggest leadership challenges within the organization for both good and bad reasons. We value age and we value maturity. Unfortunately, from the business perspective, this concept hurts us dearly if we only value age in and of itself and make a person a leader only because of age, then I say we have an issue of talent management. Like every other part of the world, we are in a talent war and in the oil industry we know technical expertise is retiring, not only here in Saudi Arabia, but worldwide. This means the backfill has been very lean. We have one of the largest capital programs in our history right now and the amount of work is phenomenal but the reserve of talent is small. It is a perfect human resource storm and can be compared to the resources bust which occurred in the '80s.

New leaders need to find people who have a strong technical knowledge base, the ability to look at the issues facing them today and in the future, and the ability to envision multiple futures. New leaders need to be able to determine what might occur and what needs to be done. They must be able to see the forest through the trees and also continue to realize that one must travel through the forest as well. These new successful leaders understand how important people are. They know that people are more than the organization's most important asset. Enablers know everyone in the company needs to be on board in order for success to occur. This new breed of leader knows how to enable individuals to work quickly and address stakeholders' needs through determination and conviction and I see new leaders as being younger leaders who have valuable capabilities, are open to new ideas, are intelligent, and can communicate well. The leaders we want are the leaders who don't perform for themselves. They perform and behave for the organization.

Corruption in leadership has been slow to become transparent in this part of the world. Within our company, we believe the more "closed" a leader is, the more the possibility increases of "bad things" happening. The more an organization opens its books and becomes transparent about its business practices, the stronger the corporation can deal with issues quickly and wisely. Internal corporate governance, ethics, and sustainability are something we will always value and practice.

Enablers deliberately tap into others' potential. They create safe environments that encourage people to speak their mind even if expressing an unpopular viewpoint. Enablers recognize that collaboration is an intellectual endeavor involving the creation of mutual goals. They facilitate discussions so that everyone feels heard and everyone understands who is responsible for the actions that develop. This type of leadership behavior creates engagement.

The Enabler helps employees become

- Fully involved in and enthusiastic about their work.
- Inspired by their work.
- Able to bring services and products to market.
- Caring about the future of the company.
- Willing to invest in the required effort to see the organization become successful.
- Conscious that the organization understands its own developmental goals and all it is doing to help employees achieve personal success.
- Connected emotionally and mentally to the organization.

The Enabler focuses on Outcomes and workforce optimization for bottom-line results. If leaders want to thrive in this competitive global market they will need to create a cohesive work environment where people feel valued and free to use their talents effectively and fully contribute to the growth and success of the organization. If leaders don't help to adapt the corporate culture to fit the needs of all people in the organization they will probably cause detrimental results in terms of hiring, productivity, retention, and creating Outcomes.

A recent non-productive behavioral phenomena is called "cyberloafing." Cyberloafing is a universal term for employees who surf the Internet while they should be working. The term first showed up in Toni Kamins's *New York Daily News* article "Cyber-loafing: Does Employee Time Online Add Up to Net Losses?" in July 1995. In 2002, Vivien Lim from the National University of Singapore wrote a paper in the *Journal of Organizational Behavior* talking about her survey of self-identified cyberloafers. Lim found cyberloafers did not loaf so much out of boredom or laziness but more as an act of defiance against what they saw as unjust actions by their employers. We want to reemphasize what we already said. If Enablers do not help to adapt the corporate culture to fit the needs of all people in the organization, they will probably achieve poor results.

The Outcomes Question

The information presented above supports the competencies of the ABL Enabler and our thinking about creating positive Outcomes. The Enabler is able to find the right blend of maximizing an individual's strengths while meeting the organization's strategic needs. A leader using this method can easily answer the question, "What Outcomes could be achieved if I engage people and leverage their talents?"

ENABLER TRAIT

#2

◭ MOTIVATION ▽

People often say that motivation doesn't last. Well, neither does bathing—that's why we recommend it daily.

ZIG ZIGLAR
American author, salesperson, and motivational speaker

Enablers are driven to achieve beyond expectations. They have a deeply embedded desire to achieve for the sake of achievement. They are motivated by the drive to achieve rather than by any potential external reward. At the same time, Enablers strive to unleash the potential of everyone they work with. Enablers communicate their passion and give a positive and hopeful outlook in achieving the purpose. They are genuine and skilled in communication.

When we talk about Motivation as a trait in the Agile Business Leader model, we are talking about:

○ What *influences* the direction in which a person is willing to go?
○ What level of *intensity* will be involved in the action?
○ What type of *persistence* is needed?

Theories of Motivation

There are some timeless theories on Motivation, all encouraging leaders to incorporate and promote the positive aspects of achieving results. Each of these theories has its own merit and each theory is relevant to the Enabler.

When it comes to Motivation, Enablers let people know their work is important and they are willing to trust that they have the competence to do their jobs. Enablers model excellence and enthusiasm for the task and encourage individuals to set ambitious goals.

One leader we worked with, his name is David, made it clear that "mediocrity will NOT be tolerated." What occurred when he set this standard was that people rose to that level of expectation and became excited and motivated by their achievements and accomplishments. By setting this expectation, David inspired his people to excel by establishing and maintaining a high performance environment. A commonly used term for this type of Motivation is "onboarding," meaning getting people on board with the concepts and actions. There are lots of theories and approaches to motivating people. An Enabler is flexible and agile in choosing the approach that reaps the best results.

What We Know About Motivated People

Leaders enlist the support and assistance of all those who are necessary to make the project work (peers, managers, customers, clients, suppliers, and citizens). They know that those who are expected to produce the results must feel a sense of ownership. One client we work with said, "My boss is like a negative energy vortex." This statement would *not* describe the Enabler. A leader who enables will form relationships founded on trust and confidence.

People are motivated to

- Enter into an unknown situation if they believe it is ultimately in their own best interest to be connected to a clear strategic vision that they can be prepared to achieve.
- Obtain desirable and pleasant consequences.
- Escape or avoid undesirable or unpleasant consequences.
- Be a valued member of a group.
- Focus on something interesting or threatening.
- Solve a problem or make a decision.
- Eliminate a threat or risk.

Undesirable Results

Motivation, like anything else, can have its pluses and minuses. Leaders know that the right kind of Motivation can increase performance and deliver results. Three researchers, Wayne Cascio at the University of Colorado in Denver and Peter Cappelli and George Taylor from the Wharton School of Business in Philadelphia, proved another outcome of Motivation that was not so positive. What these researchers discovered was documented in the *Academy of Management Journal* in an article entitled "Goal Setting as a Motivator of Unethical Behavior."

The three scientists created a situation where one group of individuals were told to "do your very best" at meeting some specific challenges. They did not have to set any goals, just consistently do their best. With the second group, the scientists encouraged them to set challenging goals and then aim at achieving their goals. An interesting twist was added to this study. All participants had an opportunity to lie about whether or not they had achieved their goals. What we found even more interesting in this experiment was that when the researchers rewarded people for meeting their goals, they cheated three to four times more frequently than those who were not rewarded. "We found that people with unmet goals were more likely to engage in unethical behavior than people attempting to do their best. This relationship held for goals both with and without economic incentives. We also found that the relationship between goal setting and unethical behavior was particularly strong when people fell just short of reaching their goals" (retrieved July 7, 2009, from http://knowledge.wharton.upenn.edu/paper.cfm?paperID=1290).

What these researchers deduced from their study was there is a strong relationship between individuals being motivated to behave unethically when they believe they will *not* reach their desired goal. These people's Motivation moves from achieving an outcome to achieving what is expected (at all costs). The study even showed that people with unmet goals were more likely to overstate the performance than people in the do-your-best condition.

For the Enabler, this study highlights the point that Motivation is closely linked to the ability of having a direct influence on results while at the same time helping people respond to issues framed in terms of losses, gains, and ultimate impact on the organization. It is true that individuals perform and respond to receiving something. Therefore, the Enabler must lead and motivate in a way that generates more alternatives, addresses individual needs, and maximizes the "exchange rate" within the organization.

An Enabler can motivate a person if that person believes

- There is a positive correlation between efforts and performance.
- Favorable performance will result in a desirable reward.
- The rewards will satisfy an important need.
- The desire to satisfy the need is strong enough to make the effort worthwhile.
- Communication is open, frequent, and transparent across all levels.

The Motivation Question

Motivating others to achieve full mind, body, and heart involvement can yield rich information for strengthening a business. The information presented above supports the knowledge needed by the Enabler and our thinking about gaining skills in Motivation. A leader who assesses a person's willingness, commitment, and Motivation levels can ensure they are on the right track to harnessing the power of the human capital. A leader with these abilities can easily answer the question, "What will motivate myself and the others to achieve at all levels within the organization and outperform the competition?"

ENABLER TRAIT

#3

LEARNING IN ACTION

It is not the same to talk of bulls as it is to be in the bullring.
SPANISH PROVERB

The ability to effectively leverage human capital is what allows organizations to catapult past their competitors. One of the best ways to accomplish this is through learning.

Learning

We define learning as a change in knowledge stored in an individual's memory that causes a relatively permanent change in that person's behavior. This change in behavior occurs because of a response to some kind of stimuli. Learning is built upon prior learning and constructing new ideas or concepts based on prior knowledge and/or experience. OK, so that sounds pretty sterile and academic. In reality, leaders help people think to think or learn to learn. For us, learning has become exciting over the years as people start to become more agile and discover and invent new ways to share information and help others learn. A story we came across while writing this book emphasizes how this occurs, even though how we learn is changing.

On February 7, 2009, at Henry Ford Hospital in Michigan, surgeons removed a cancerous kidney from a sixty-year-old man using highly sophisticated 3D robotics through a single incision. That is quite a feat in itself, but what does it have to do with learning, you might ask. What makes this surgery so interesting to us is that this kidney surgery was broadcast live using Twitter, the free micro-blogging service. Doctors uploaded short play-by-play messages, or "tweets," to 385 Twitter users, directly from a laptop in the darkened operating room. Doctors also answered questions (in real time) from the Twitter users about the surgery. Who would have thought Twitter could improve medical learning?

High Points in the Chronology of Learning Concepts

At this point, we thought it might be helpful to highlight a historical perspective on learning. If, as a society, we are able to teach about a kidney surgery in one part of the world to learners in another part of the world, how did learning begin? The following list is a history trip down "learning lane." This is by no means intended to be a comprehensive list. Rather, it is intended to highlight years of key learning concepts with a mixture of learning theories by category:

i) Behaviorism: a learner is essentially passive and responds to environmental stimuli.
ii) Cognitivism: a learner is viewed as an information processor (like a computer).
iii) Constructivism: a learner is an information constructor.
iv) Design-based: learning is a complex system of general or predictive theories of learning.
v) Humanism: learning is viewed as a personal act to fulfill one's potential.

We believe a learner is only as intelligent as the degree to which that person is aware and in control of her or his thoughts, actions, and choices. If you subtract these three things, you have a stifled learner. Therefore to promote this ABL Learning in Action competency, an Enabler must

• Foster learning goals.
• Encourage organizational commitment to allowing people to actually learn.

- Offer leadership development opportunities.
- Place an emphasis on management to promote learning.
- Promote the "onboarding" process of getting the "buy-in" to ideas and building loyalty to the cause.

One leader told us, "Life is a silly little concept and there sure is a lot of learning that's going on during it." We agree with this leader and know that learners are motivated to learn only if they determine the meaning and value of an experience, and information they receive, can be valuable to them. This concept became all too true for Eileen while she was driving her eight-year-old son Bryan to his first day of school in second grade.

Things You Can Learn at School

THE OTHER DAY MY SON MADE ME REALIZE that some valuable skills can be learned in school. As I drove my son, Bryan, to his first day of second grade, his face shone. He had his new backpack, new lunch box, new haircut, and new clothes. He was ready to learn and experience all that school had to offer him. Now Bryan is someone who is hungry for knowledge. It is not enough that the toast pops up from the toaster; he wants to know all the exact details of how it happens. He is not satisfied that the water runs down the drain, he wants to know exactly where it goes and why. No matter how involved or gory the details are, Bryan wants to know them all. This desire for details is unlike my daughter, who, when she was eight years old, learned pollen is essentially plant sperm. "Ahhhhhh," she screamed, "I'm breathing sperm!!!!!!" At which point, after learning about this natural process, she refused to take a breath outside for three weeks. "I don't want to breathe sperm," she said. She also did not want to learn any more details on the topic.

Bryan was different in his craving for learning. His mind kept working well after his eyes were closed and the lights went out for the night. This is why it came as no surprise to me, while in a carpool line waiting to start that first day of second grade, Bryan said, "You know,

Mom, it's real egocentric of people to build robots that look like humans, when they could function better if they were really designed for the job they had to do."

"I never thought of that, Bryan." (Which I might add, had become my standard answer.) As Bryan got out of the car, I hoped school could help him learn and gain the knowledge he craved. I also hoped his teacher would have an answer to the robot question before "pick up" time. This was in the days before the Internet, and I was lost at where to find out why robots are built the way they are.

In the afternoon, I picked Bryan up from school and was interested to see what the education system had offered him in the way of learning. As Bryan threw his backpack and lunch box into the car, he leaped into the front seat with a big toothless smile and his shoulders thrown back as if to show off some sort of badge on his chest. "Mom," he said bursting with excitement. "Guess what I learned today?"

Ahhh, the moment of truth, the answer to why we are so egocentric to make robots like humans. "What did you learn at school today, Bryan?" "I learned how to burp my name!" And from that very important social learning insight, now I know you can learn a lot of useful skills when groups of people come together!

Learning is more than understanding the past. Learning used to be based on the proposition that knowing how people did things in the past was adequate preparation for doing well as a learner in the present. In 2010, we propose that the concept of learning can no longer be an approach where knowledge and skill are "pumped" into a person the way traditional learning has done in the past. Whatever the age of the learner, a teacher/leader must direct the learner's involvement and must relate the learning directly to real issues of the here and now. This new direction of learning must create the capability within people to leverage their strengths to their advantage, while at the same time intentionally address their weaknesses.

Think to Think

It might come as no surprise that within organizations these days, people have more to learn, greater access to information, less time to learn, and greater expectations placed on them professionally and personally.

For these reasons Enablers teach individuals *how* to think, not *what* to think. Enablers move beyond an emphasis on leadership development and begin to stress knowledge transfer, broader skill building, and just-in-time learning. They go beyond considering learning as a conscious act, involving logical reasoning and stressing self-control. Instead, they expand their promotion of learning to include

- Abstract thinking.
- Problem solving.
- Third-person thinking to consider different points of view.

At the heart of this ABL competency is Learning in Action, which encourages the approach of giving the learner the opportunity to choose "whether and what" activities he or she will engage in and learn. This means, in the process of Learning in Action, the learners get to decide the meaning and the value of their experiences.

Developing Learners

To really begin to engage a learner, the Enabler must develop within the learner the following three criteria for learning: courage, truthfulness, and acknowledgment. The Enabler helps a learner develop the following

1. Courage

Learning Action: Relinquish control and take risks to deal with uncertain information and engage in creative inquiry.

Enabler's Role: Help learners feel comfortable with being uncomfortable and comfortable with learning new things.

2. Truthfulness

Learning Action: Encourage the absence of hypocrisy, inventing, falsifying, embellishing, or exaggerating current information or reality.

Enabler's Role: Help learners reduce the need to protect their ego and being confined by self-consciousness and social acceptance.

3. Acknowledgment

Learning Action: Be honest with yourself. Attempt to understand as clearly as possible what you are experiencing and undertaking. Perhaps accept, if just for a while, the idea or concept is true and become motivated to move forward.

Enabler's Role: Help the learner temporarily accept the present and become open to possibilities to determine if he or she will embrace the learned concepts.

Leading and Learning

Optimum productivity and human satisfaction can't be reduced to rules and formulas, whether grounded in economics, engineering, or human relations.

Kahlil Gibran, the Lebanese poet and painter, said, "The teacher, if indeed wise, does not bid you to enter the house of their wisdom, but leads you to the threshold of your own mind" (*The Prophet*, Chapter 18, "Teaching" [Bracken Books, 1994]).

The Enabler involves people in

- Setting important goals.
- Structuring opportunities to learn.
- Offering feedback and support.
- Providing tools and ideas for learning.
- Maximizing opportunities for individual or group learning.

The funny thing is, there is no demonstrable connection between intellectual power and business success. What does provide inroads to business success is how an organization develops sustainable learning environments for everyone to positively impact the bottom line.

How to Build a Sustainable Learning Environment and Promote Learning in Action

- Engage top leaders in learning.

- Invest in learning in good times and bad.
- Integrate different learning strategies.
- Know that people can learn to become self-correcting.
- Energize learning behavior by rewarding it when it happens.
- Recognize that learning happens at all levels in the organization.
- Emphasize the learner's interests, personal ability, and prior knowledge of the topic.
- Create opportunities to support collaborative learning that is learner controlled.
- Maximize the learning potential by helping learners develop individually achievable objectives based on their interests and abilities within the context of what needs to be learned.

The Learning in Action Question

We are sad to report our experience with clients has been that most businesses are anti-learning and have no tolerance for mistakes. The information presented above supports the competencies of the Enabler and our thinking about Learning in Action. A leader with these abilities can easily answer the question, "How can I provide a setting for innovative learning that promotes participation, anticipation, and a norm of working together?"

ENABLER TRAIT

#4

COLLABORATIVE CULTURES

In the long history of humankind (and animal kind, too)
those who learned to collaborate and improvise
most effectively have prevailed.

CHARLES DARWIN

When we use the term "culture" we are talking about the deep-seated attachments to "the way we do things around here." An organization's culture includes all the behaviors that are determined by the long-held formal and informal systems, rules, traditions, thoughts, and customs. It has been our experience that a person can learn about a company's culture by looking at its values, norms, routines, rituals, as well as artifacts found decorating the area. You can also tell about a culture when you hear people say, "This is the way we do things around here." An organization's culture has a strong influence on the behavior of the people over time. When cultural differences are not understood and appreciated, people tend to stereotype and discriminate. When employees are in sync with an organization's culture you typically find a high retention level, increased productivity, and increased overall job satisfaction.

A strong Collaborative Culture is the common denominator among the most admired successful companies around the world. We are not talking about non-Collaborative Cultures that are loaded with "micro meddling" and people colluding politically. Instead Collaborative Cultures view dialogue and building an environment for commitment as the key to sustainability. Collaborative Cultures embrace bottom-up processes.

Building a Collaborative Culture provides

- Opportunities for mutual growth.
- Engines for personal development.
- Alternatives for thinking and behaving.
- Tools for building and improving relationships.
- Methods for considering possible solutions and new approaches.
- Forums for richer decision making.
- Opportunities for shared leadership.

The concept of leaders creating Collaborative Cultures is not new. In fact it can be traced back a hundred years to Frederick Taylor, a mechanical engineer who is considered to be the father of scientific management. In 1890, Taylor showed factories how cooperative values and having everyone work together in unison can solve workplace problems (even if workers had limited expertise).

It was Taylor's strong set of personal beliefs that drove his thinking about building Collaborative Cultures. Taylor's mother and father were

Quakers, members of a religious society that believes the Inner Light in each person provides direct access to God without intermediaries or literal readings of Scripture. Quakers value the principles of peace, equality, integrity, and simplicity. Taylor's father was a lawyer and his mother was a feminist who helped run an Underground Railroad station for runaway slaves in the United States. It was this mix of values passed down to him from his parents that caused Taylor to embrace peacekeeper values and make an effort to resolve conflicts in the workplace.

Taylor could not imagine one leader/person having all the qualities needed for the job. He did not believe one person could have education, physical abilities, strength, energy, confidence, honesty, common sense, and good health all at the same time. With this thinking in mind, Taylor divided up the leader's role into tasks and functions. This was radical thinking in 1890, yet Taylor persisted with his thinking. Taylor thought a "specialist" would learn faster and do a better job. He encouraged leaders to be the "servants of the workmen." He said a leader's role was not to order people around; instead, a leader's role was to discover the one best way to get the individual to work.

The result of Taylor's thinking was the building of Collaborative Cultures in the 19th century because workers no longer depended on the leader for answers; instead they began to trust each other and rotate leadership roles based on relevant skills and knowledge. Taylor not only used the values of his upbringing as a Quaker for his thinking on building cultures, he also borrowed his ideas from the Egyptians who built the pyramids by breaking tasks into their smallest components and setting daily production quotas. For Taylor a Collaborative Culture had the ability to get tasks organized right the first time and produce outstanding results.

As organizations move toward the 22nd century, breaking tasks into small components and into small departments has caused silo disciplines and attitudes to occur. With silos, only chunks of performance are being optimized and significant results are not happening. Individual production pods with the goal of collaboration cause individuals difficulty because of

- The temptation to maximize personal gain.
- The difficulty in giving something up that a person created or owned.
- The fear of being taken advantage of.

A real-time example commonly used to show these stifling effects of collaborating in silos is something now called the "Lordstown Syndrome." In 1969, General Motors (GM) management redesigned their plant in Lordstown, Ohio, in order to transform it into the most modern, competitive, and sophisticated assembly plant in America. This new initiative was in response to the global challenges posed by low-wage labor in modern West German and Japanese automobile factories. In 1969, the Lordstown automobile plant produced the Vega 2300, a small car intended to compete against the Volkswagen Beetle, Ford Pinto, Toyota Corolla, and Nissan Datsun.

Leaders for GM collaborated on their thinking and increased job efficiency through reorganization and better coordination between the car body and chassis assembly lines. The leaders improved controls over product quality and worker absenteeism by making the jobs at the plant more simplified and automated. Although tasks were already simplified, leaders further divided the work into the smallest possible units, and created narrow, repetitive tasks that intentionally did not allow the workers any flexibility. The new design relied on greater automation and less on human effort to reduce error. In addition, the design also reduced performance of a task from the typical one minute down to 36 seconds.

What the GM leaders did not consider in their collaborative efforts for efficiency was the human capital side of their performance initiative. They did not consider, when they rolled out the new plan, "what relation will workers' performance have to the new approach to automation?" Because the question was not asked, in 1971, the workers, the human capital at the Lordstown plant, began to intentionally drop nuts and bolts into car engines to cause inefficiency in the system. They also neglected to anchor parts to the car body, because of "the stress and frustration over having to complete a task in 36 seconds or less."

When you dig deep to understand these dynamics, at the heart of these deliberate sabotaging techniques was the buildup of employees' anger about work conditions. They believed the new requirements caused a lack of opportunities for personal independence and growth. The lesson from this event: although the working environment might have seemed to be collaborative, the leaders did not take into consideration the needs of the workers, the human capital of the organization.

When a leader's cultural priorities and values focus only on the business capital to the exclusion of the human capital the results can be

1. Dishonesty, resulting in
   * employee theft (goods and time)
   * untruthful communication

2. Absenteeism, resulting in
   * workplace safety hazards
   * illness
   * stress
   * low energy and motivation

3. Sabotage, resulting in
   * intent to do damage
   * rejection of innovation
   * threats of possible risk

What this means in a world of massive information and technology is that leaders must become more agile in their thinking and consider every angle of a situation. They must understand the importance of information sharing and value human capability and engagement.

This concept of Collaborative Cultures is so important to people these days that there are now many websites created to let anyone share their thoughts about their place of work. For the Agile Business Leader, this adds a whole new dimension to the meaning of Collaborative Cultures. One example of what we are talking about is JobVent. JobVent is a website where anyone who wants to find out what the culture of an organization is like or wants to see what current employees are saying about a company can find the desired information. The website has been set up with the belief that this is valuable information for anyone wanting to consider working for the specific organization. It should also be pointed out that all the postings on the site are anonymous, which can certainly change the way people present their opinions.

The following is an entry from JobVent that clearly does not indicate that the person giving his or her opinion on their company thinks he or she is working in a Collaborative Culture.

> 04/24/2008: Certainly one of the poorest managed companies I've ever experienced. The executive management is way too young and inexperienced and has never worked in any significant roles for other companies, so they only know one way to manage—through fear & intimidation. They install branch managers and expect them to turn a branch around in 60 days or they're pretty much out the door. Talk about cheap? This company expects its employees to scrub the toilets, change the light bulbs, sweep the floors, etc. You name it. They are too cheap to out-source to a 3rd party. Probably could be a highly successful company if the CEO would get out of the way, hire some outside executive management and spend more time developing employees. (Retrieved June 6, 2010, from http://www.jobvent.com/reviewDetail.php?ID=26729)

OOCH! Not the nicest review of an organization. From the perspective of the Agile Business Leader it is worth thinking about the following:

1. What would happen if your actions were subject to public review?
2. How could you behave more as an Enabler and encourage Collaborative Cultures?
3. What style of leadership would work best in your organization and with your human capital?

The new reality for organizations and for leaders who are saying they want to establish a Collaborative Culture is that of public and anonymous feedback. Whether a leader likes it or not, creating silos within the organization, designing procedures into small tasks, and building compartment-type management structures can no longer be the predominant way of "how things are going to be done around here." Building a Collaborative Culture must be based on reciprocity and the message that the long-term benefits of collaboration outweigh the short-term benefits of not cooperating. In the end, collaboration will *only* work when everyone believes the leader is authentic in his or her efforts. Then the leader is positioned to enjoy the benefits of collaboration from the "human capital" in return.

Enablers' Natural Resource

Enablers know that their main natural resource is the curiosity of the people around them. With this human capital resource they can begin, create, and sustain collaborative environments that support rapid "onboarding," or getting the "buy-in" from individuals involved. Building upon the curiosity of people means the leader can scale up retention and engagement efforts along with improving talent management. What this means for Enablers is that when they develop a collaborate environment they create a willingness for others to be cooperative and they start to eliminate the fear a person might have of being taken advantage of. Enablers focus on shared goals because working toward these goals together is far less stressful than pursuing them individually.

In every Enabler's life there will be setbacks. We are not so naïve to think otherwise. What is unique to Enablers is that they treat setbacks as opportunities for growth and learning.

David Spann is a colleague of ours. He is also the president of Agile Adaptive Management. We thought it would be appropriate to ask David about being an Agile Business Leader since he works with agile concepts and helps leaders and organizations become more "agile and adaptive" by creating better performing teams, providing executive coaching, and facilitating strategic planning programs.

David expressed these thoughts on leadership.

THE DEFINITION OF BEING A GOOD LEADER depends on which level of the organization you are talking about. This is particularly true in the area of software development. When software needs to be developed, tested, and designed, working together as a team and being a collaborative leader is very important. In this kind of situation, being a good leader depends on a person's ability to enable people to achieve results. If a leader took a traditional leadership role in this case, he would kill the creativity of the people involved.

When a person is leading at a level above the development of software, he has to have more passion and has to be focused on the mission of the business and not just on the business of team building. He needs to know how to make the business run smoothly. He needs to understand the vision, purpose, and potential of the company. Working well with people is part of that.

All leaders need to understand the
1. Methods required to achieve results
2. Environment that needs to be created to help people succeed
3. Approach for improving and increasing the flow of work
4. Expected outcomes needed to be addressed at each level
5. End-to-end processes for
    i. How things work
    ii. When things get handed off
    iii. What friction exists
    iv. Understanding which people are effective in getting things done

In my view, one of the biggest challenges of leadership is having and using the skills of collaboration and letting go of your personal needs. A leader needs to help people to do their work and to work well together. He can do this by trusting the group involved in the task. This is different from traditional leaders who have been trained to be the "expert" and have their people follow them because of it. This type of leader uses more of a "do as I do" philosophy to leading.

You can identify agile leaders because they engage people in the purpose and mission of the organization and they engage the people they work with well. I am also aware that being a good leader and an agile leader is not always easy. In 1989, I experienced one of my most challenging moments as a leader. It was June 28 in New Meadow, Idaho, and I had just started a new job as a district ranger. I was thirty years old and was considered a young leader for the job. Frankly I was scared to death because of the enormous responsibility placed on me. On July 11 (thirteen days from my first day on the job) the state of Idaho had one of its traditional thunderstorms. These thunderstorms were accompanied by lightning strikes that started 211 fires overnight. Of the 211 fires, 89 of those fires had started in the district I was responsible for. Talk about being a leader who was being "tested by fire"!

In the job, the process for dealing with fires was clearly defined. You had to make out a "Request Order Form" for fire resources to be sent to your district. Typically as a district ranger, you might have one fire at a time and you would make the request saying you need these specific resources to manage this one fire. Well, on July 11 at 5:00 am (and my second week on the job), I telephoned the resource group for the district and said, "I don't know you and you don't know me but the thing is I have a major crisis here with eighty-nine fires burning all at the same time. What should we be doing and what could you do for us?"

We talked and planned all day. In addition, every morning for the next six weeks, I led two thousand firefighters to join forces and work together to extinguish the fires. We were the tightest team in the area and we got things done. Even more important, we did not lose one life in the process.

When I think about what made this team a success, I'm reminded of the six team-building components Patrick Lencioni describes in his book entitled *The Five Dysfunctions of a Team*; these are very similar to leadership philosophies or values instilled in most firefighters:

1. *Trust:* I had to trust the people I worked with or fire them and find someone else to work with.

2. *Communication:* We held daily debriefing sessions to get everyone in line. We continued that format during every fire season from that point forward.

3. *Camaraderie:* We laughed a lot and sometimes we drank a lot after our shifts were over.

4. *Celebration:* When the fire season ended, we played and celebrated our successes.

5. *Unselfishness:* I asked for what we needed and nothing more. In the world of government we made a deal with ourselves to only use the resources we absolutely needed and we became proud of that philosophy.

6. *Truthfulness:* We told the truth even though it was painful. We figured you have to face the danger; don't run away from it or it will kill you. So we faced the danger and we faced the consequences of speaking truthfully.

When I take the learnings and the values from my experience as a leader, and think about the common characteristics that need to exist for all leaders, I would say there are five essential skills leaders need to be Agile Business Leaders and enable people to do their best work.

1. *Focus on Results:* When a leader allows more time for conversations and gives the patience of time, good things emerge.

2. *Assure Accountability:* Giving feedback and expecting accountability are critical as a leader. By engaging people and developing processes for gathering, analyzing, and taking action on the information, a leader can help people learn how to do it better next time. Leaders coach people to continually learn from and be accountable for their actions.

3. *Insist on Commitment:* When people believe passionately in a common purpose, that passion can change the world. My experience is that you won't end up with a 50/50 situation if you have commitment. Instead, you end up with everyone on board.

4. *Engage Conflict:* When a conflict exists, a leader uses consensus decision making, the process of passionate debate, to build engagement in the group. That engagement then ends

up in a committed pathway forward for everyone. The pathway also begins to create more passion, engagement, and commitment between group members.

5. *Rely upon Trust:* Leaders must trust the wisdom of the group even if they do not agree with the decision. I keep being reminded of that truth every time I forget to do it.

David was quick to tell us that Agile Business Leaders must develop a business culture necessary to support agile practices and assure that an organization's strategy, project portfolio, and the tasks of individuals must be aligned with and focused on the business purpose. We would add that as a leader leads and builds the commitment required to sustain incredible outcomes, she or he also develops collaborative business practices to reduce the types of behaviors that get in the way of success. Some might say in David's job as a district ranger he managed and controlled the fires in the state of Idaho. Today we often think that our colleague David has a great talent for putting fire under people to make them higher performers!

Using Collaboration to Maximize Human Capital

Collaborative environments launch organizations into the world of economic success. We have been working with the architectural firm Aedas for many years. We facilitated our first program for Aedas in 2001 when they were a good quality architectural firm with 130 employees who primarily focused on the Hong Kong infrastructure sector. By the end of 2009, they had become the second largest architectural company in the world with 2,500 employees collaborating across 31 countries. This extraordinary growth and success were led by the efforts of Aedas's chairman Keith Griffiths and his CEO, David Roberts.

This company has shown phenomenal growth over the past few years. Aedas has implemented many initiatives that leverage the power of collaboration across the business and the communities in which they work. Their internal collaboration crosses geographical and functional boundaries and their external collaboration involves universities, charities, and community organizations. As Aedas has grown so too have their people and the communities they support.

Conditions for Creating Collaborative Environments

In whitewater rafting the boat does not have a rudder yet the crew somehow works together to steer the boat through the rough waters. There is a lot to be learned from what it takes to make that happen. Enablers are often a bit like the leader of the raft. Their team works together to get through the rough waters by

- Sharing all relevant information with stakeholders and creating more accurate decisions.
- Continuously examining the processes that build and maintain the collaborative environment.
- Valuing differences in the opinions, values, and ideas of others.
- Promoting open, honest, and trusting communication.
- Encouraging the development of knowledge and competencies by creating environments conducive to learning.
- Providing frank and direct feedback to let people know how successful they are.
- Blending information, logic, and emotion into decisions.
- Using inclusive language: *us, our, ours,* and *we* versus *me, my, mine.*

These processes are critical in creating a Collaborative Culture. Like the name implies, the leader must lead the cause of collaboration, which includes incorporating all different views and perspectives. Perhaps you have heard the Jain story, of *The Blind Men and the Elephant.* Jainism is a religion founded in 550 BCE. Its doctrine is rather unique because it involves the promotion of "change" and "persistence" all at the same time. This "one reality" Jainism promotes is something called *Anekāntavāda,* or "the theory of many-sidedness." In the story of the blind men, the idea of looking at something from different views and perspectives can produce something stronger than only looking at something from one perspective. For those readers who are not familiar with the story we include it below.

SIX BLIND MEN WERE ASKED to determine what an elephant looked like by feeling different parts of the elephant's body. The blind man who feels a leg says the elephant is like a pillar; the one who feels the tail says the elephant is like a rope; the one who feels the trunk says the elephant is like a tree branch; the one who feels the ear says the elephant is like a hand fan; the one who feels the belly says the elephant is like a wall; and the one who feels the tusk says the elephant is like a solid pipe. A wise man explains: "All of you are right. The reason every one of you is telling it differently is because each one of you touched the different part of the elephant. Actually the elephant has all the features you mentioned."

We include *The Blind Men and the Elephant* story as part of this Enabler competency to emphasize the concept of collaborative interactions and valuing the different perspectives and truths each person brings to the bigger picture. The story has been used over the years to show that "reality" may be viewed differently depending upon one's perspective and that the absolute truth may be relative due to the deceptive nature of half-truths.

The Collaborative Cultures Question

Enablers realize the value of encouraging diverse thinking and plugging into the unlimited intelligence of the people within the organization. They know when people work together in unison and create alignment with respect and honor, innovation and sustainable results follow. A leader using this trait can easily answer the question, "How can I ensure I am collaborative to maximize the results of everyone involved?"

CONCLUSION TO ENABLER

As for the future, your task is not to foresee it, but to enable it.

ANTOINE DE SAINT-EXUPERY
French writer, aviator, and author of *The Little Prince*

Enablers have had the mind shift from seeing people in organizations as machines to one of considering people as human capital who, when enabled, can transfer information more effectively and respond to clients' needs faster. They build on the natural strengths of the human capital to build outstanding results. There is a story told by the Danish philosopher Søren Kierkegaard linking the enabling human capital's natural strengths and building on an individual's characteristics.

> ONCE UPON A TIME, a man who lived in Denmark would feed a flock of wild ducks every fall before they flew south for the winter. After a few years some of the ducks changed their migration path choosing to stay in Denmark and not be bothered to fly south. Instead, they wintered in Denmark and fed on what the man continually gave them. After three years, the ducks grew so lazy and fat that they found difficulty in flying at all.

Kierkegaard's moral to this story: "You can make wild ducks tame, but you can never make tame ducks wild again. Once tamed, they begin to never want to go anywhere again."

Enablers do not "tame ducks"; instead they let them flourish. They build environments within organizations for "ducks" to be wild and therefore provide the best talent and ability imaginable to the organization. When Enablers act with honesty, integrity, and a sense of responsibility to employees, their customers, the community, and other stakeholders, individuals become proud to work for the enabling leader.

When leaders understand, embrace, and build processes and practices to embed values-based qualities into their organization's culture, they most often delight all stakeholders. This culture will positively enhance the customer experience, help leaders exert greater influence over a highly decentralized global workforce, lower costs, and boost revenues. We cannot overemphasize the need for leaders to see the potential greatness in their own people. We encourage all leaders to look for the latent potential within every person.

The business leader who is prone to put mental straitjackets on people will confine them to a role or a job description without truly envisioning what they are capable of. As we were writing this book, we did not find many textbooks or guides on how to operate as a global business in a world that is dealing with strained economics, diverse cultural beliefs, political unrest, and increased competition. Our recommendation for enabling people in this global economy is to

1. Build consensus for change by positively introducing a vision backed up with validating data.
2. Communicate how people can contribute to the organization and what progress is being achieved.
3. Create positive motivation instead of negative consequences by asking people what motivates them and then celebrating small successes with quick rewards.
4. Assemble a strong team to keep engagement alive.
5. Identify talent needs so that you can recruit and hire better people each time you fill a vacancy.
6. Build communication bridges between generations at work.
7. Give people real authority and full information to do the job they were hired to do.
8. Achieve full support and backup from upper management by being transparent in business operations.
9. Practice "knowledge care" instead of "knowledge management" as a new leadership paradigm.

As we conclude this chapter, we are reminded of a story that emphasizes the extent to which a leader's actions and decisions can affect the performance and productivity of an organization. It is a story about when a leader does not consider all the elements of enabling the human capital of the organization.

The Story of the Tea Lady

One of our clients, a large construction company doing $5 billion USD worth of business in Hong Kong, needed to cut costs during some difficult economic times. On one particular morning, we contacted our client for a follow-up telephone call and learned that in the last month the morale in the company had plummeted. It wasn't difficult to find the cause of the problem.

In Hong Kong, it is common for companies to continue the old British tradition of having a "tea lady" employed by the company. The tea lady is a woman whose job is to provide beverages (tea, coffee, water, etc.) to employees and visitors. She works full-time serving tea to staff and visitors at every meeting. Now the tea lady usually gets to know everyone and knows everything that is going on in the organization. What upset our client and the morale in this organization was the fact that they found out the tea lady had been sacked as a cost-cutting measure. What the bosses didn't realize was that she was the unofficial morale booster and confidante in the office. "She was like the caring mother who was always happy and interested in us. She knew about families and knew how to make us feel comfortable. When they sacked the tea lady the rest of us thought, 'What does this company value?' I mean her salary really didn't impact the company that much but the effect she had on our morale was monumental. Leadership doesn't seem to have its priorities straight."

When the staff within an organization doesn't understand the company's direction or feels disassociated from the decision-making process, they lose the energy and motivation to contribute. People judge leaders by their actions, not their intentions. We tell our clients, "You may have a heart of gold but so does a hard-boiled egg." What is inside the leader counts, but if it cannot get out through actions, then it can never contribute to the success of others. When people within an organization experience the feeling being valued and included, engagement and performance naturally increase.

Confucius might offer some of the greatest wisdom for this Agile Business Leader trait. Confucius suggests five qualities essential to perfect virtue, saying:

TO BE ABLE TO PRACTICE FIVE THINGS everywhere under heaven constitutes perfect virtue; seriousness, generosity, sincerity, diligence and kindness (*Analects*, bk. xvii., c. vi.). If you are serious, you will not be treated with disrespect. If you are generous, you will win all hearts. If you're sincere, you will be trusted. If you are diligent, you will accomplish much. If you are kind, you will enjoy the service of others. (*Analects*, bk. i., c. viii., v. 1.)

Leadership is all about the release of human possibilities. One of the central requirements for good leadership is the capacity to inspire people in a group: to move, encourage, and pull them into the activity and to help them get centered, focused, and operating at peak capacity.

Enablers show leadership by inspiring others to act. They demonstrate and value collaboration and mutual learning by leveraging talent and enabling people to perform at their best. Being an Enabler simply means making the most of the organization's human capital.

Ideas in Action

Enabling people toward action in multinational, multicultural workforces demands an ability to get everyone motivated and aligned to the same strategy. In 2001, the executive team of Aedas, a good quality Hong Kong architectural practice, wanted to improve their performance. The managing director, Keith Griffiths, contacted us and suggested that Aedas's board of directors were simply seven good architects and wondered if we help do something about molding them into an effective board without losing their architectural expertise. That phone call began an 8-year program of development with Aedas that saw them rise to 2,500 people across 31 countries and become the second largest architectural practice in the world.

This transformation was led by the now CEO David Roberts, a master enabler and master salesman. David achieved the massive change by relying on his ability to get people motivated to succeed, to share the vision he had, and to constantly and tirelessly "care and feed the environment he was creating." The Cartaphor on page 131 was developed in 2004 and was used to explain Aedas's business development strategy and the role everyone in Aedas should play to ensure their vision became a reality.

This Cartaphor depicts Aedas's business environment as a war zone. The narrative that accompanied this Cartaphor explained each strategy within the war zone metaphor.

Using this type of image and explanation was a very effective way to get the message across in a multilingual, multicultural environment using the simplicity of a metaphor and the "visual innocence" of a cartoon.

QUESTIONS TO CONSIDER

These questions are designed to challenge some of your current thinking and to practice a new communication process. If something in the Cartaphor does not work for you, change it; this is simply designed to tap into your creativity and build your ability to relate complex issues in a simple way.

Imagine yourself represented as an Enabler in this Cartaphor as you answer the following questions.

1. If you were in the Asia war room, what messages would be appropriate to the send to the troops to ensure a collaborative approach for achieving actions?
2. What positive messages can you generate from the Cartaphor that will motivate people toward action?

3. How can you use the diversity in your organization as a valuable asset for the "Battlefields of Tomorrow"?
4. How can you enable people and change the environment to maximize learning?
5. Which piece of this Cartaphor could be used to foster better communications in your organization?
6. What will be the best way to build trust given all the elements involved in this Cartaphor?

PERSONAL ACTION PLAN

Self-assessment and adaptability are extremely important as an Agile Business Leader. We suggest you devise a personal plan to accomplish changes you want to implement for yourself or your organization. Ask the question, "What actions or changes in my behavior do I need to accomplish and by when?" Then construct an Action Plan that will help you achieve your goal. Write it down and monitor it or use your community of practice to help you become even more accountable for your actions.

Action Plan

	Action Item	Resources Required	Date of Completion
1			
2			
3			
4			

What actions or changes in my behavior do I need to accomplish? How soon?

_____

_____

_____

4

THE CHAMPION

❖ *Demonstrates Capabilities* ❖

If you don't stand for something you might fall for anything.

ALICE COOPER
Lyric for his song "Stand"

I n the role of Champion, a leader responds to the realities of needing to be people-focused and at the same time, needing to have the
capabilities to perform. The Champion focuses on helping the group
dynamics of the organization by positively focusing on current and past
strengths, successes, and potentials and at the same time, mobilizing
and incorporating his or her own talents to achieve the end results.

The four traits of the Champion are

❐ Resourceful
❐ Responsive
❐ Resilient
❐ Committed

In the role of Champion, the ABL recognizes that speed and responsiveness have become more important than ever for business survival. Getting people excited about performing quality work, staying committed
to the cause, and moving forward toward profitability are major components for overall success. Champions are responsive, authentic, and willing to expose themselves by having the courage to do what is right. They
get excited about the possibilities that new ideas can bring. Champions
personify corporate values and help form the character and the strength
of the organization. They have the courage to stand up for what they
believe and have a strong orientation toward achievement. They have
high expectations for themselves and for others and always push to
achieve. In short, the Champion's role is about the leader's character.

Personifying a Champion is a leadership component that is all but
forgotten by modern standards. Traditionally, corporations value leaders who are rational, strategic thinkers who develop excellent systems.
This old way of thinking valued people who *ran* the organization. Today, organizations need Champions who continually *create* the organization as it responds to ever-changing business demands. Creating an
organization and leading people successfully are achieved by a leader
with a strong character, confidence, and courage.

THE NEED FOR CHAMPIONS

We know through our work that people have become the driving force of business success. When we talk to our clients and other global leaders about what makes an organization successful, from the perspective of its people and their capabilities, the overwhelming response we hear is "leadership quality impacts success." It is the leader who creates value for stakeholders and is adaptive in responding quickly to customers' needs. Leaders who are trustworthy and courageous to make the "tough calls" are the ones who earn the respect of people following them.

We have heard it said that if you want to find out how good tea can be then put it in hot water. The same is true for Champion leaders. You can tell how good Champions are by the way they deal with crises, ethical issues, and attacks on their character and by their need to stand up for what they believe is right.

Champion leaders have existed throughout history. You might have heard stories about great leaders who fostered innovation, built commitment, engaged the masses, and aligned people to the vision. In the book *The King Alfred Millenary: A Record of the Proceedings of the National Commemoration*, the English novelist Sir Walter Besant talks about King Alfred as being a model for great leadership. He states, "There is none like Alfred in the whole page of history, none with a record altogether so blameless, none so wise, none so human. He is truly a leader" (p. 8).

When we read this excerpt it catches our attention. What made King Alfred a great leader? Through an agreed period of time, he is thought to be the greatest forefather in terms of wisdom, competence, and moral nobility. Upon further investigation, we learn that he became famous for his courage and skill as a warrior. King Alfred valiantly defended England against a stronger enemy, the Vikings and the Danes. He understood the value of diplomacy and formed amicable relations for securing peace. Alfred was also devoted to the welfare of his people. He rebuilt structures, imported foreign scholars, founded schools, and personally learned Latin in order to translate books into English so his people could improve their literacy. He assisted people in learning. We agree that accomplishing these feats makes a leader great. We also know that a lot of these characteristics are incorporated today in capabilities of the Champion.

Champions present themselves to the world as confident, adaptable, responsive, and perseverant people. They have an intense work ethic, are disciplined, and are unruffled by provocations. They are dynamic ambassadors who consistently maintain integrity, overcome resistance, and promote a unity of purpose. They assume strategic responsibilities and their contribution to the growth of the business can be easily identified. They understand they have value. The Champion has the wisdom and innovation to work cross-functionally by influencing, inspiring, and leveraging optimization and utilizing the strengths of the organization. Champions have the courage to try out new approaches and do what no one else does. They are worth watching and emulating.

It is our belief that Champions are ordinary heroes who do extraordinary acts under the right circumstances. They know what is expected of them and have the confidence to be innovative in whatever way they can to get the job done. They are the people who have both skill and will to do the right thing at the right time, in the right way, and for the right reason. In a way, the Champion's role could be considered a global currency for business because the capabilities possessed in this area are valued around the world.

The case for becoming a Champion is compelling since speed in anticipating and responding to customer demands and quality in delivering results continues to be an important ingredient of competitive advantage. Champions have the passion to strive and surpass their personal goals because they have the capability for relentlessness and consistency.

CHAMPION TRAITS AND COMPETENCIES

The ABL Champion integrates four traits with seven competencies to leverage a unique market position and sustain future growth. The seven Champion competencies along with the competencies of the Specialist, Strategist, and Enabler include the following:

Resourceful:
1. Use innovation practices to influence and adjust.
2. Build internal and external networks.

Responsive:
3. Understand self and use strengths.
4. Set high expectations.

Resilient:
5. Practice work/life balance.

Committed:
6. Act with courage.
7. Achieve with self-determination.

The following sections of this chapter describe how each of these competencies supports the four traits that define the Champion's role.

CHAMPION TRAIT

#1

⚜ RESOURCEFUL ⚜

Supreme resourcefulness consists in knowing the value of things.

FRANCOIS DUC DE LA ROCHEFOUCAULD
French writer

Being Resourceful is different from using your resources. Being Resourceful centers on being able to make the most of a situation with the immediate amenities you have at hand. Resourcefulness incorporates perspective, innovation, and the ability to create solutions in a way that may be different from the usual.

The well-known artist M.C. Escher pushes people to perceive things differently. In one of his famous lithograph prints entitled *Relativiteit*,

M.C. Escher's "Relativiteit" © 2010 The M.C. Escher Company—Holland. All rights reserved. www.mcescher.com

Escher depicts figures ascending and descending through a series of windows and doorways surrounded by gardens.

The person looking at this artist's work is challenged by contrasts, dualism (reality consisting of two opposing principles), transformation, infinity, and spatial absurdity. The picture emphasizes a person can focus on the unusual result—in this case walking up stairs that go nowhere. For us the picture emphasizes our belief in leaders needing to be open and willing to consider any conflicting points of view in order to succeed. These are the capabilities used by the Resourceful Champion who is not limited by imposed ideas and beliefs. Resourceful Champions know how to expand the possibilities of the experience because they recognize that it is all in how they interpret the situation and what they want to focus on.

One Canadian leader we know, named Howard, told us the story about being Resourceful and the need to be very focused on a moose-hunting trip. The story is not directly related to leading within an organization. At the same time it certainly draws on many scenarios business leaders face and provides an excellent metaphor for operating within those realities.

I SET UP A NICE CAMP on a small point of land that the moose frequent and started to hunt. On my right was the north shore. I saw the three moose, and straight ahead to the west about a hundred yards was the mouth of the Wanipigo River. I started to blow my moose call. Almost immediately, I heard a howling on the far shore. I continued to blow the cow and distressed calf calls (these are the calls used to lure a bull into range). I heard the howling increase in volume and number. I knew it wasn't a moose but couldn't resist this interaction with the wild, so I continued my moose call. The howling continued and moved closer until all at once, a pack of ten wolves appeared on the shore a hundred yards across the water from me. They all ran around the shoreline straining to look over the water at what I assume they thought was a moose in trouble (that "moose" would now be me). They were all white/gray wolves, and they were big! A pack of ten wolves moving as a unit with the intent of hunting is a bit disconcerting. I was about a four-hour paddle from home and literally up a creek from the nearest human. I realized I had only three bullets in my gun with little opportunity to reload if the wolves decided I was a reasonable moose substitute. My canoe was well up on shore and could not be put in the water in the couple of minutes it would take for the wolves to close ground. I decided to stop calling (good move I thought) and made myself visible to the pack. I reasoned (thinking this could be my last thought) that given the time of year (it was October), that the pack couldn't be terribly hungry. If it was February, things would be different. I also reasoned that wolves will usually avoid humans unless they are very hungry. The pack saw me and stopped their pacing as they decided what to do. I took aim, to be ready, should they make the wrong decision. If the pack moved to the right, that would indicate that they were taking the shortest route around the water to come to where I was. I would have started shooting to scare them off or at least reduce their numbers before they got to me and my machete (my last line of defense). Fortunately they moved off to the left which, given the landscape, indicated they were going elsewhere. I was glad they did, and I didn't shoot. I couldn't help but think that an attack by a wolf pack in a remote area must be a scary and probably fatal thing. These animals are big (larger than a large German Shepherd) and there were ten of them moving in a coordinated fashion. If they had attacked and persisted, I figured I could have shot three and maybe taken two or three with my machete, but I would never have gotten them all. I was amazed at how quickly they came to the moose call and how organized they were. I never did get a moose during this hunting trip, but I sure had a great time. I did realize it pays to be Resourceful and

use whatever resources you have in the situation you are in, in this
case, my gun and my machete. Even more, I realized the importance of using your mental Resourcefulness to think through the issues from every angle. I had to calculate how hungry the wolves
were based on the time of year, decide to stop using my moose
call and assess how the wolves might behave and what their decision would mean for determining my best plan of action.

We can honestly say we are not big fans of camping vacations where the
definition of success is that you have to survive. Yet, we are big fans of
Champions being Resourceful, both mentally and physically. The story
about Howard speaks about the Resourcefulness that any Agile Business Leader needs to work within organizations. It addresses the point
about using or not using your tangible resources (tools and equipment)
and your intangible resources (your intellect and experience) under pressure. *"I took aim, to be ready, should they make the wrong decision."*
The Champion is alert and ready. The Resourceful Champion accurately assesses the situation, calculates the risks involved, quickly assesses the best plan of action, determines how to best use the tools
available, stands confident while implementing the plan, and learns
from the adventure.

Most people don't see the world as it is; they see it as they are. The
Resourceful Champion sees the bigger picture.

Being Resourceful involves

1. Suspending judgment and having healthy skepticism.
2. Thinking of outrageous (and practical) possibilities for designing
   workable solutions (in some cases for one's own survival).
3. Experimenting with different perspectives when assessing situations and resolving issues.
4. Going against conventional wisdom and societal norms when addressing challenges.
5. Taking stock of what is available and applying it toward the
   solution.

The Resourceful Question

This list for showing what is involved in being Resourceful supports the competencies of the Champion and our thinking about competencies for Resourcefulness. A leader who is Resourceful can easily answer the question, "What other resources do we need to incorporate for creating a solution to this situation?"

CHAMPION TRAIT
#2
RESPONSIVE

It's not the strongest species that survive,
nor the most intelligent, but the ones
most responsive to change.

CHARLES DARWIN

With competitive pressures limiting a company's ability to raise prices, Responsiveness is one of the few remaining business growth sources. Being Responsive brings a kind of speed and agility to an organization that can be leveraged into an even greater competitive advantage. Responsiveness involves being decisive and having the ability to make and to act on difficult decisions swiftly and well. It also means acknowledging and understanding the needs and priorities of another person, whether a client, a vendor, or someone working within the organization. Champions are willing to respond to the situation and use their talents in the best possible way. They are prepared for uncertainty and unplanned events because they know the reality of the current "on demand" business and operating environment.

Responding to demands is greatly affected by the Champion's attitude, stamina, and ongoing learning. Champions have the ability to focus and to share knowledge and ideas in order to improve processes and products. This is what makes a Champion Responsive. In some cases, responding to demand means you have a different opinion today than you did yesterday. However, this could also be perceived negatively as being "wishy washy" or too political. We contend it relates to adaptable thinking and is used as a means of striving to constantly stay abreast of the altering needs of people and situations by being flexible, fluid, and free. We are also recommending that leaders let people know why their position is different at any point in time from it was before the triggering event.

Mohandas Gandhi regularly changed his mind—often publicly. An aide once asked him how he could so freely contradict this week what he had said just last week. The great man replied that it was "because this week I know better." We want to make the point that Responsive leaders are willing to adapt and evolve into situations by changing their position and their way of doing things.

A Responsive leader is a person who is able to identify both the explicit and implicit needs of the people she or he interacts with and uses the understanding of those needs to try and fulfill them, whenever required. Champions are generally interested and concerned about the well-being of their people. They are more than willing to work together and less likely to be callous or indifferent. Champions have the ability to identify needs and priorities and act upon them in a direct and consistent manner. They are always ready to accept responsibility. Because of this, they are respected, trusted, and perceived as reliable and useful to the organization.

In this "on demand" global environment, Responsiveness has become an issue of customer demand, global supply, talent and flexibility, for satisfying customers' unique and changing needs. The explanations below expand on these four areas.

1. Respond to customers' demands: Understanding the customer's inventory levels, ordering patterns, path to profitability, and unique business challenges will allow Champions to serve their customers better. If you really listen to your customer, you will know exactly what your customer is saying, and you will be able

to better explain how your product or service is of value to that particular customer. Quickness in anticipating and responding to customer demands is an important ingredient of competitive advantage. Customer-centric strategies keep the business focused on big-picture goals that can truly build value for your organization.

2. Identify global supply: Champions have the optimal mix of local and overseas suppliers and can respond better to the fluctuations in their business. Understanding which ones are the right suppliers helps with sourcing materials to keep the costs down, reducing long lead times and allowing the project to change at a moment's notice as the situation requires.

3. Maximize use of talent: Champions know that success lies in the ability to build respect and trust among the people they interact with. When people can communicate well, regardless of geographic boundaries, leaders can begin to help increase productivity and Responsiveness. This means Champions must give their team members quick access to whatever resources are currently available. When geographically dispersed staff needs to collaborate, Champions respond by taking advantage of communication tools such as e-meetings, virtual whiteboards, and portals. Champions include analytical, emotional, and communication skills to ensure they are able to respond positively, effectively, and with agility.

4. Provide business flexibility: You can't be Responsive to customer needs with a "one size fits all" strategy. The ability to reconfigure business processes quickly and accurately, produce quality work, and meet deadlines is important in a world of unprecedented business and market pressures. To meet business needs and "on demand" requirements, Champions integrate open, efficient, customer-centric infrastructures.

The Responsive Question

The list above supports the competencies of the Champion and our thinking about being Responsive. A leader with these abilities can commit to providing both customers and employees with the best service and support available, respond more quickly, increase productivity, optimize assets, and grow revenue, even in an environment of moderate growth. A leader in the Champion role clearly articulates the desired outcomes and focuses on productivity, operational excellence, competitive differentiation, and creation of contingency plans. Champion leaders are achievement-focused and take initiative. They can easily answer the question, "How can I be more Responsive to customer requests and effectively handle the most complex orders quickly, efficiently, and accurately?"

CHAMPION TRAIT

#3

▲ RESILIENT ▼

The reasonable man adapts himself to the world; the unreasonable one persists in trying to adapt the world to himself. Therefore, all progress depends on the unreasonable man.

GEORGE BERNARD SHAW
Irish playwright and socialist

Traditionally, leaders are paid to be right. In turn, they have a vested interest in making sure their opinions prevail. Most often these traditional leaders do not take pleasure in being contradicted. In our experience we have found that leaders (especially traditional ones) are annoyed by disagreements or resistance. Unfortunately this restrained approach is exactly the opposite mindset needed for a leader to achieve in today's business environment. Leaders can no longer "just tolerate" diverse thinking; they must actively seek it and think as a Resilient Agile Business Leader.

The concept of Resilience has to do with the ability to bend, stretch, compress, and return back to your original shape or position. For example, after being stretched, a rubber band returns to its original shape when the tension on it is released. Being Resilient, as a leader, means being able to bend, stretch, and *absorb change gracefully while retaining core values and functions.* The qualities of agility and flexibility enable leaders to be Resilient and recover quickly and reliably when they are stressed or thrown off balance by change or adversity.

Resilient leaders draw on their ability to be optimistic, which allows them to function well in difficult situations. They have an abundant reserve of centeredness, innovation, and stamina.

Being *centered* refers to being emotionally stable and secure. It is this centeredness that enables leaders to keep balance when turbulent times knock them around. When ABL leaders are centered, they are poised and level-headed, especially under stress. They feel calm, composed, and completely present.

Being *innovative* refers to the ability and power to create solutions of value. When leaders are innovative they express themselves with imagination and originality. They envision new possibilities and respond to novel situations with flexibility and improvisation.

Having *stamina* refers to the physical and moral strength required to sustain prolonged stressful efforts or activities along with the ability to withstand hardship or adversity, disease, or unexpected change. When you have an abundance of stamina, you feel invigorated and confident in your ability to endure.

Resilient leaders who are centered will be innovative, and their stamina increases their capacity to thrive regardless of the situation swirling around them. Champions are able to recover quickly from illness, change, or misfortune. The ability to perform and thrive under conditions of ambiguity and uncertainty is essential for the Resilient Agile Business Leader.

From a biological perspective, humans are quite Resilient. When we get frightened our body gives us a shot of performance-enhancing hormones and pumps blood to our limbs to help us outrun whatever enemy we face. It has been found that people who respond well to trauma and are Resilient to the adversities of disasters tend to have three underlying advantages:

1. A belief that they can influence events.
2. An ability to find meaningful purpose in life's turmoil.
3. A conviction that they can learn from positive and negative experiences.

Champions recognize their natural ability to be Resilient and can adapt in the face of adversity, significantly influencing the situation and alleviating the sources of stress. They are able to bounce back from workplace and personal stressors.

Eileen remembers the story of one of the most frightening experiences of her life and how she quickly learned to be Resilient during and after experiencing danger.

MY MOST FRIGHTENING EXPERIENCE was when I was a cashier at a department store and a man came in, held a sawn-off shotgun up to my face, and demanded money from the cash register. I was nineteen years old at the time and working during the Christmas holidays at a large retail store. The area of the store where I worked was packed with people, and the man with the gun began yelling at me to put the money in the bag. Clearly I did not want this man to harm anyone. He was agitated and nervous, and I knew terrible consequences were possible. As I began to open the cash register, he screamed louder, shaking the shotgun in my face and demanding that I hurry up. I began to talk to the man smoothly and calmly (I have no idea how I did that), saying that I would do as he asked and he would get what he wanted. I removed the money from the drawer and filled his bag. The people in the store looked with horror as the event unfolded. The man took the bag, turned around with the gun pointing in the air, and demanded that no one should move. Immediately after the man left, I called the police and then checked with the customers to make sure everyone was all right. After the police came, we reviewed mug shots, and they commented on my calmness and ability to capture some of the details of the robber. I was on a mission to catch this person and knew providing every bit of possible information to the police would be helpful in apprehending him. After the robbery and review of all the mug shots, I went home. It wasn't until I was sitting on my couch in my home that I began to shake when the internal realization of what had happened hit me. Somehow, during the events of the robbery, I was able to communicate effectively, keep people calm, perform under stress, and manage strong feelings and the impulse to scream and pass out. The next day I was back at work, wiser and more alert to my surroundings. We also put new procedures in place to help manage how much money was kept in the cash register at any one time.

The concept of Resilience is about the ability to bounce back quickly. How much Resilience a person has at any given moment can make the difference between a leader experiencing a particular situation as painfully challenging or as an open-ended opportunity for personal growth—or even an adventure. In dealing with and managing turmoil, a leader must act quickly. Resilience under the threat of turmoil or chaos is a function of speed, decision making, action, reaction, collaboration, and swiftly applied common sense. Timidity and hesitation are not options. Truly Resilient leaders do not just recover and return back to exactly what they were before the chaos occurred. Instead, they add to their knowledge reservoir and increase their Resilience capability.

The key to staying successful as a leader, despite the challenges and chaos in business, is finding ways to bounce back. Resilient leaders are able to solve problems with a calm, confident sense of being able to overcome adversity. They approach challenges with agility and learn from each experience (both positively and negatively).

We recommend the following approaches for developing Resilience:

Focus on succeeding

- Focus on opportunities, not obstacles.
- Expect that good things can happen despite adversity.
- Exert positive influence to create positive outcomes.
- Be clear about what matters most.
- Stay focused—value-driven, not event-driven.
- Solicit feedback to understand reality from multiple perspectives.

Strengthen mental abilities
- Renew physical energy through periodic recovery time.
- Develop emotional empathy and self-awareness.
- Learn greater self-control to manage strong feelings and impulses.
- Expect the world to be disruption-filled.
- Learn to steady concentration to manage adversity.

Expand thinking
- Build and maintain supportive and positive relationships.
- Develop the capacity to make and implement realistic plans.
- Evaluate and affirm strengths and abilities.
- Enrich skills in communication and problem solving.
- Increase ability to respond in a positive and decisive manner.
- Develop a high tolerance for ambiguity, paradox, and complexity.
- Celebrate small wins.

The Resilient Question

The list above supports the competencies of the ABL Champion and our thinking about being Resilient. In the role of Champion leaders who have this competency do not use it to get bogged down and chained up by restrictions; instead they become more Resilient and able to quickly bounce back from any disruptions that might occur. They have the ability to be flexible, step back to gain perspective, be more adaptable, and rebound well from diversities. Building the habit of Resilience helps a Champion to elegantly weather the unavoidable ups and downs of the business environment. The Champion is Resilient and will seek out new opportunities even in times of crisis, easily answering the question, "How can I bounce back from periods of stress and times of chaos?"

CHAMPION TRAIT
#4
⚜ COMMITTED ⚜

There is no action without desire, for it is desire that causes us to act.

ARISTOTLE

Organizational Commitment and optimism are fundamental to Agile Business Leaders. In our experience, we find that *Commitment to the organization* has a great consequence for business and, more important, can be strongly impacted by the way leaders work with employees. The old psychological contract between an organization and employees, the one where employers provide job security and predictable advancement to employees in exchange for their loyalty and performance, has been damaged beyond repair. Organizational Commitment is being challenged by employees who are more attached to their profession than to their organization and apply greater discretionary effort on what and whom they will be committed to.

This ABL trait of Commitment is about attachment to a cause, including its goals, values, and purpose. We believe Commitment affects a leader's performance on the job, his or her intent to leave or stay on task, and the amount of effort he or she is willing to put toward an outcome. An impressive example of how Commitment can strengthen an outcome is the story of W. N. Murray.

Murray was an avid Scottish mountain-climbing enthusiast who joined the Scottish Division of the British Army during World War II. While in the war, he spent three years in prisoner of war camps in Italy, Germany, and Czechoslovakia. With Commitment and passion for mountain climbing, Murray wrote a book about it while in the terrible conditions of the war camps. He wrote his book, *Mountaineering in Scotland*, on rough toilet paper, which was the only paper he had available to use. His manuscript was found by the Gestapo and destroyed.

Murray did not give up hope. He was Committed to his cause, and to the surprise of his fellow prisoners, he started to write the book again.

After the end of the war, Murray's Commitment not only helped him publish his first book, but several others as well. He is known in history as the person who rejuvenated the postwar interest in mountain climbing. Not only did Murray write his edition, but he was also a deputy leader to the climbers on a Mount Everest expedition. Unfortunately, Murray failed to acclimatize to the altitude and was no longer included on the successive teams. Being unable to achieve a dream did not stop Murray from sharing them with others through his writing. In one of his books, Murray writes about Commitment and the courage to continue with the cause even when things seem lost. His lessons are very relevant to the Champion:

> BUT WHEN I SAID THAT NOTHING HAD BEEN DONE I erred in one important matter. We had definitely committed ourselves and were halfway out of our ruts. We had put down our passage money—booked a sailing to Bombay. This may sound too simple, but is great in consequence. Until one is committed, there is hesitancy, the chance to draw back, always ineffectiveness. Concerning all acts of initiative (and creation), there is one elementary truth the ignorance of which kills countless ideas and splendid plans: that the moment one definitely commits oneself, then providence moves too. A whole stream of events issues from the decision, raising in one's favor all manner of unforeseen incidents, meetings and material assistance, which no man could have dreamt would have come his way. I learned a deep respect for one of Goethe's couplets:
>
> Whatever you can do or dream you can, begin it.
>
> Boldness has genius, power and magic in it!
>
> (W. N. Murray, *The Scottish Himalayan Expedition*, 1951; retrieved February 19, 2010, from http://www.goethesociety.org/pages/quotescom.html)

When Commitment exists and a leader believes and accepts the goals and values of the purpose, then that leader is willing to exert considerable effort on behalf of the cause and the organization. But where does Commitment come from and how can you achieve it?

There is a theory that Commitment level is based on a biological effect within a person. Psychologist Peter Hall of Waterloo University in Ontario, Canada, found a connection between Commitment and behavior that lies in the neurons of the brain (more specifically, the prefrontal cortex, which is the front of the brain, located right beneath the forehead). The cortex is responsible for mediating conflicting thoughts, making choices between right and wrong, helping you decide on a defined goal, and having social "control" to manage outcomes. During his research, Hall gave participants the "Stroop" test, an electronic test in which names of colors flash on the screen for an instant, but are aligned with the "wrong" colors. For example, the word "red" would be written in green letters and the word "blue" would be written in yellow letters. The purpose of the test is for the person to quickly identify the color of the letters. The test is difficult, because to answer correctly a person has to mentally override his or her impulse to read the word. This same effort to override what one reads is what is needed for Commitment. A person must use his or her mental capacity to stay focused on the task and create the habit for follow-through and Commitment. This ability for follow-through and Commitment also requires self-regulation and the ability to do things that are not immediately rewarding, or do things that are more or less uncomfortable or even simply inconvenient. This means being Committed is not easy. Biologically, Commitment requires a healthy mind (or prefrontal cortex) and something you want to Commit to.

Organizational Commitment comes in three varieties:

1. Normative: The desire to conform. A sense of obligation to the company and the extent to which an individual identifies with the specific work tasks and responsibilities that make up the job.
2. Economic: The desire to avoid the cost of leaving. A connection based on the cost associated with leaving the current situation for future work and career.

3. Emotional: The desire to have an emotional attachment to an organization for whatever reason. A connection to the psychological strength received when working with the organization.

Leaders often wonder just how Committed they should be to an organization. In the 1972 Academy Award–winning film *The Godfather*, Michael Corleone (the youngest son of Don Vito Corleone and head of the Corleone crime family) turns to his brother as the ruthless boss and says, "It's not personal, Sonny. It's strictly business." If what we now know about Commitment remains true, then leadership is not "strictly business." It is personal, because leaders must be personally Committed to what they are doing to achieve the results they desire. Complete separation between business and personal affairs does not exist because we are more than the body we bring to work each day. The leader's entire person is at play when focusing on Commitment. Being a Committed leader to an organization will depend in part on

- Leadership effectiveness and supervision.
- Work environment.
- Adequacy of the technology and resources available.
- Compensation and benefits.
- Teamwork and work process effectiveness.
- Communications and decision making.
- Job content and satisfaction.
- Work/life balance and flexibility.
- Diversity of thinking.
- Ability to perform and advance in learning.
- Culture aligned to personal values.

There is substantial research that supports the claim that organizations with more Committed employees outperform in sales and financial performance. Committed employees stay at their company longer, work harder, and deliver "on-brand" work every day. They do this because they are more satisfied, productive, and active in serving customers. They are more confident and agile in their thinking and will calculate risks and pursue new opportunities more fully.

The Committed Question

This discussion supports the competencies of the Champion and our thinking about gaining Commitment. A leader with these abilities can easily answer the question, "How can I enhance my Commitment and in turn enhance shareholder value?"

CONCLUSION TO CHAMPION

Championship is a leadership component that is all but forgotten by modern standards. Corporations tend to value leaders who are rational, strategic thinkers and system developers. They value the people who run the organization. We suggest that the Champion creates the organization. The Champion's role is about the character of the leader. It is about the essence of who the leader is as a person. It goes beyond actions. If values are the soul of an organization, then the Champion personifies those values and characterizes the strength of the organization through personal character.

We propose that Champions have four specific character qualities to become a valuable asset to any organization. These characteristics are critical to the future success of any organization.

The four traits of the Champion include being

1. Resourceful.
2. Responsive.
3. Resilient.
4. Committed.

Many people pay lip service to the idea that leading an organization requires strength of character. We claim character is central to being a leader. The character of a Champion includes the emotional fortitude to be honest with oneself, with others in business, and with the realities of the organization. Champions are open to whatever information they need, whether it is what they like to hear or not. They have the courage to accept points of view that are the opposite of theirs and to deal with conflict. They have the strength to accept and to deal with their own

weaknesses and the courage to be firm with people who are not performing. They can handle ambiguity, which is so inherent in a fast-
moving, complex organization. The multitude of characteristics included in this chapter encapsulates what makes up the character of the
Champion. In the words of Warren Buffett, a successful investor, philan-
thropist, and one of the richest men in the world, "The road that leads
to great success is usually paved with a ton of mistakes, so get over it
and on with it. If you don't like leading, you can always follow." The
Champion likes to lead and has the character to lead in an exemplary
manner.

Ideas in Action

The Cartaphor below was used with GroupM to help all employees understand their valuable Championship role in the company. GroupM is
a multinational media group that, at the time this book was written,
has 402 offices in 81 countries and employs 14,000 staff. Mark Patterson is the CEO for GroupM Asia Pacific. As the leader, Mark wanted to
explain the organization's vision, values, and complex interrelationship
structures to every person in the business. There are several different
businesses within the group, so the need to ensure everyone understood
how the group works together was important and greatly needed for
the business.

As mentioned earlier in this chapter, Champions get people excited
about performing quality work, staying Committed to the cause, and
moving forward for profitability; these are major components for success. Champions are authentic, and they showcase their excitement
about new ideas by personifying corporate values and characterizing
the strength of the organization. They have the courage to stand up for
what they believe and have a strong orientation toward achievement.
They have high expectations for themselves and others and always push
to achieve.

Mark and his senior management team decided to represent the vision, values, and culture of GroupM using the cartoon/metaphor of a
music festival. They felt that in order to be more culturally relevant to

the dynamics of their operational environment, they would encourage employees to perform as though they were at "GroupM Fest." Leaders wanted everyone to value the fundamentals of respecting individuality, having fun, being successful, pioneering new concepts, and seeing the benefits of the power of one. Like the traits of the Champion, they wanted people to have the courage to stand up for what they believe and have a strong orientation toward achievement.

To further push the concepts of Resourcefulness and innovation, Mark and the other leaders decided to animate their Cartaphor into an interactive digital platform. This meant that everyone viewing the concept could "play with" different ideas to learn all about the culture, the values, and the interrelationships between the different businesses. By scrolling over a section, the interactive component of the Cartaphor would emerge. Using these innovative practices to influence and adjust how people think and engage is exactly what a Champion does. Champions not only think about building their internal and external network, but they help others do it as well. They set high expectations, act with courage and achieve results through self-determination. They are a Champion at the "Fest" and enjoy when others are as well.

QUESTIONS TO CONSIDER

The following questions are designed to increase your awareness and challenge some of your current thinking. They are designed to help you develop a more agile mindset. Imagine yourself represented in the Cartaphor as a Champion as you answer the following questions.

1. Who represents you at this music festival and why?
2. Who are the other characters at your festival and how can you all work together to form something great?
3. If other actors are performing better than you on their stage, what could you innovate as a solution to increase your effectiveness?
4. What area of this festival are you most Committed to help to achieve and why?
5. What are your expectations for the festival?

6. What could this festival do to become more successful?
7. How can you manage, lead, and coordinate all the acts at this festival?
8. What area of this festival requires you to exert the most amount of personal courage?

PERSONAL ACTION PLAN

Self-assessment and adaptability are extremely important as an Agile Business Leader. We suggest you devise a personal plan to accomplish changes that you want to implement for yourself or your organization. Ask the questions: *what actions or changes in my behavior do I need to accomplish and by when?* Then construct an Action Plan that will help you achieve your goal. Write it down and monitor it, or use your community of practice to help you become even more accountable for your actions.

Action Plan

	Action Item	Resources Required	Date of Completion
1			
2			
3			
4			

What actions or changes in my behavior do I need to accomplish? How soon?

5

THE SPECIALIST

❖ *Incorporates Expertise* ❖

To know how to use knowledge is to have wisdom.

CHARLES H. SPURGEON

The Specialist responds to the realities of needing to be business focused and at the same time having the capability to achieve. Specialists are focused on helping the business grow its technical, profit,
and governance capabilities.

Four traits make up the role of the ABL Specialist:

❏ Industry Knowledge
❏ Operational Intelligence
❏ Specific Expertise
❏ Corporate Accountability

Specialists aggressively hunt and gather ideas and opportunities before
others are even aware of the need. They study trends and technological
developments and are focused readers. They are sponges for information and experiences. They know that a highly diverse and broad base
of knowledge and experiences will enable them to assimilate novel ideas
and connect seemingly unconnected pieces of information. They are
quickly able to analyze a situation, make decisions, and act on opportunities. They search out new ways to form shortcuts to slash red tape.

Specialists use their role to gain knowledge, expertise, and wisdom.
They use the collective intelligence of those around them. They strive to
continually grow their knowledge and expertise base and convert it into
value for the organization.

THE NEED FOR SPECIALISTS

As authors we were honored in being co-named *Time* magazine's 2006
Person of the Year. We were chosen "For seizing the reins of the global
media, for founding and framing the new digital democracy, for working for nothing and beating the pros at their own game." And the good
news is, you were chosen also! In 2006 *Time* magazine made a controversial decision to name every Internet user "Person of the Year." They
believed "you control the information age" and therefore the honor was
justified. The story's lead author, Lev Grossman, has said this award is
"a story about community and collaboration on a scale never seen before. It's about the cosmic compendium of knowledge Wikipedia and

the million-channel people's network YouTube and the online metropolis MySpace. It's about the many wresting power from the few and helping one another for nothing and how that will not only change the world, but will also change the way the world changes." What this new community-focused and collaborative approach will do is to help create useful short cuts, slash red tape, and assimilate novel ideas.

There is no denying the "revolutionary change" that *Time* magazine acknowledges is real. Web 2.0 is just the beginning. (Web 2.0 is where the World Wide Web is integrated with computer applications—for example, getting the maps you need off Google Earth or walking around with a GPS receiver in your phone.) Web 2.0 provides new interfaces, user-created data, customer self-service, and new ways to search and access the Web for content. By its very design, it builds community, social networks, and ownership as people share data over their devices.

As for leaders, revolutionary change is about adapting to the "Digital Natives", the new generation who are growing up on the Web. They are living with Podcasts, blogging, Mashup [programs that combine data or functionality from two or more external sources to create a new service], Life-hacking, Citizen Media, Collective Intelligence, and Wiki. It would appear that today's leaders are not only faced with the challenges of globalization, they are also faced with "googlization." What does this mean for the ABL Specialist who must work within this *"cosmic compendium of knowledge"* in a change and be changed world? A world where *you* "control the information age"?

Increasingly, globalization influences everything around us. New ideas and diverse cultures are becoming a more integral part of our day-to-day existence. The leaders we work with realize that if an organization is not willing to embrace technology, be open to diverse means of receiving information, grab ideas, and be adaptive to change, it will not survive.

To work among these changing global strategies, the ABL Specialist values knowledge gained from formal learning experience, reasoning, expertise, judgment, and insight. As the pace of change increases in business, the value of the role of Specialist increases at the same rate. If you want to assess how critical Specialists are to the success of any business, think about how much of their leadership role depends on their knowledge and therefore what would be the full cost of replacing that person.

The competencies of an ABL Specialist have become a leading commodity for economic success. In his book *The New Knowledge Organisation*, Charles Sigismund writes: "Because knowledge does not wear out and people can duplicate it practically without cost, knowledge is a source of super value and super productivity. Knowledge alone can add value to an otherwise closed, zero-sum system" (*The New Knowledge Organisation* [SRI International, 1995], p. 11). Since knowledge has become a hot commodity, it is no longer acceptable for a leader to simply have normal cognitive abilities. Today it is essential for the leader to have the ability to reason, solve problems, perceive relationships, and store and retrieve information.

If organizations are to succeed in an economy where small insights can quickly shift the competitive edge and where capabilities can rapidly be bought, borrowed, or built, then an organization's intellectual capital (employees' brainpower and know-how) must be valued. Each organization must form a clear sense of what characteristics promote and nurture the best leaders within the organization.

Tim Smith, who was president of Vonage Networks (a leading provider of VoIP Internet broadband telephone services), told Eileen the story about the early days working with the organization.

THERE WERE ONLY ABOUT FIFTY PEOPLE working for the company when we began to get a lot of customers and a lot of traffic on our network. One day the NOC (Network Operations Center) began to overheat. If it got too hot the entire system would shut down and that would be the end of our service. One of the engineers came to me and told me about the potentially devastating situation. I turned to him and said, "Get me a hammer and a fan." There were a lot of concerned looks on people's faces and I yelled again, "Get me a hammer and a fan!" They brought me an axe and I immediately began to smash a hole in the wall to let the hot air out of the room. I put the fan in the NOC to help blow the hot air out. The temperature dropped immediately and the system did not fail. That afternoon the CEO Jeffrey Citron walked by the hole in the wall and the fan blowing and yelled out, "Who did this to the wall?" No one wanted to take ownership. Someone said, "Tim Smith did it. The NOC was about to overheat." Jeffrey looked at the group and said, "This is exactly the type of thinking we need around here! We need people to use their heads and react to situations so our customers don't lose service. Great plan!"

What Tim Smith did was use traits from his ABL Specialist skill set to resolve the crisis.

Today, the knowledge economy is calling for leaders to have "metacognition" abilities (a higher order of thinking that involves the capability of knowing whether or not you know). Metacognition involves having the ability to acquire knowledge, manage knowledge, monitor comprehension, and evaluate progress, as well as change and adapt business strategies as needed.

In the role of an ABL Specialist, the need for metacognition requires leaders to be more agile in their thinking and know

1. What: has knowledge and understanding of industry characteristics and trends.
2. How: comprehends trade secrets, best practices, and best processes for delivering exceptional results.
3. When: able to present information in a timely matter (recognizing that intelligence diminishes as time lags).
4. Who: able to locate the key people who know what to do and how to do it.
5. Why: able to comprehend and understand the real issues and contribute to an accelerated pace of technical and scientific advancement in order to assume an advantage over competitors.
6. Where: able to navigate networks or systems accurately and maximize business impact while optimizing the use of available resources.

ABL Specialists use metacognition and perseverance to effectively apply and distribute knowledge throughout the organization. They build flexible organizations that reduce waste and increase productivity by integrating thinking and doing at all levels.

SPECIALIST TRAITS AND COMPETENCIES

The ABL Specialist amalgamates four traits with the following five competencies in order to leverage a unique market positioning and sustain future growth. These five Specialist competencies along with the competencies of the Champion, Strategist, and Enabler dictate that leaders have the following:

Industry Knowledge:

1. Understand industry trends.

Operational Intelligence:

2. Build quality systems.
3. Build a reservoir of internal and external operational expertise.

Specific Expertise:

4. Consistently update their specialist knowledge.

Corporate Accountability:

5. Exemplify corporate governance.

SPECIALIST TRAIT

#1

⚜ INDUSTRY KNOWLEDGE ⚜

To know that we know what we know, and to know that we do not know what we do not know, that is true knowledge.

COPERNICUS
Polish astronomer

Industry Knowledge, if applied appropriately, is a powerful force. It is a key catalyst for progress. It can transform business and have an enormous impact on stakeholders. It seems there is a galloping complexity in deciding what to know and what tactics one should have in order to respond appropriately to the forces of change that are ever present. It is apparent in today's business world that the amount of knowledge available to any person capable of using the Internet, for example, is constantly growing.

The ABL must be curious and constantly searching to gain more knowledge and insight. This point reminds us of a story about a young man who took off on a long and dangerous journey. He was searching for a wise old man who could give him the answer to the age-old question, "What is the meaning of life?" After many days of travel he finally found the wise man and asked him his question. "Sir, what is the meaning of life?" The old man replied, "Life is just a bowl of cherries." At first, the young man was stunned and speechless. Then he became annoyed and angry. With great frustration, the young man turned to the wise sage and said, "That's it? I've come all this way, over oceans, over mountains, through deserts and jungles to seek your knowledge and ask you, 'What is the meaning of life?' and all you have to say to me is that 'life is a bowl of cherries!" The old man smiled, adjusted his robe, and looking very wise turned to the young man and said, "All right, so life is not just a bowl of cherries."

We tell this story to emphasize the importance of personal perception and our ability to go beyond what is usually thought of as our "boundaries" in gathering knowledge and achieving. When leaders try to expand their Industry Knowledge, a great deal depends on the interpretation of the information received. As human beings, we want to search for the absolute truth and are less comfortable with ambiguity. When it comes to gaining Industry Knowledge, understanding the meaning and significance of the information is entirely dependent on your interpretation of the information received. In fact, the more you expand your thinking and become more agile in your approach to synthesizing information, the greater your sphere of knowledge will become.

Specialists do not just search for knowledge; they investigate information to create insights and understanding. They determine who has the knowledge, who needs the knowledge, and who knows how to convert the knowledge gathered into valuable information for the business. The Specialist continually searches what is happening in the industry and thinks of ways to take action for increasing the probability of success for the business.

Ashleigh Brilliant, an American author and cartoonist, says in one of his cartoons: "There has been an alarming increase in the number of things I know nothing about" (PotShot #0729). In this situation, the Specialist recognizes that it is critical to know his or her industry inside and out. Specialists must be aware that there is certainly an enormous amount of information they still need to know and are not foolish enough to think they know it all. Specialists continually use all their resources to gain concise clarity on a situation. This is done because they know it is the leader's knowledge that helps create, improve, advise, deploy, and develop solutions. Having this combination of experience and Industry Knowledge enables the ABL to pick up a financial statement and immediately see where a company is making or losing money. It can also allow a sales representative to translate a customer's need into a business opportunity.

The organization Teleos is an independent knowledge management and intellectual capital research company. Each year Teleos presents the

"Most Admired Knowledge Enterprises" (MAKE) program. The review panel is made up of Global Fortune 500 senior executives and knowledge management experts. They search for candidates from Asia, Europe, Japan, and North America and find "MAKE Winners." In their view, the list of knowledge performance dimensions that lead to achieving superior business performance includes

- Creating a corporate knowledge-driven culture.
- Developing knowledgeable workers through leadership.
- Delivering knowledge-based products/solutions.
- Maximizing intellectual enterprise capital.
- CCreating environments that welcome knowledge sharing.
- Creating a learning organization.
- Delivering a value base for customer knowledge.
- Transforming enterprise knowledge into shareholder value.

The managing director of Teleos, Rory Chase, says, "Organizations that effectively transform enterprise knowledge into wealth-creating ideas, products, and solutions are building portfolios of intellectual capital and intangible assets that will enable them to out-perform their competitors in the future."

Teleos's list of performance drivers closely supports components of the Specialist and our thinking about Industry Knowledge. They include performance drivers that take the organization in the right direction, help to make the right decisions, and improve operations and profits (retrieved February 19, 2010, from http://www.businesswire.com/portal/site/home/permalink/?ndmViewID=news_view$newsID=2008120905054&newsLang-er).

The ABL Specialist understands the value of knowledge sharing, teamwork, informal learning, and joint problem solving. These alliances are advancing the innovative capabilities of the organization and driving new intellectual property.

The Industry Knowledge Question

A leader with Industry Knowledge can easily answer the question, "What are the key factors for competitive success in our specific industry?"

SPECIALIST TRAIT

#2

⏶ OPERATIONAL INTELLIGENCE ⏷

> Only the extremely ignorant or the extremely
> intelligent can resist change.
>
> SOCRATES
> Greek philosopher

Operational Intelligence includes the techniques and methods for optimizing business processes and identifying and acting on patterns and
bottlenecks that negatively impact the accomplishment of the strategic
objective. The objective of having Operational Intelligence is to deliver
meaningful information to individuals so they can make quick, accurate, well-informed decisions. Tools that aid Operational Intelligence
include real-time data on business processes, systems, and structures.
These tools allow data and information to be made available to any
user, at any time, and can be used for re-establishing best practices, increasing the speed of decision making, and addressing mission-critical
situations as they emerge.

Operational Intelligence within an organization can be found in the
form of innovation systems, intelligent data-capturing processes, and a
culture that rewards responsiveness and achievement. Today, organizations commonly use and gain Operational Intelligence through Web 2.0
technologies, including wikis, blogs, mash-ups, simulation applications,
chat rooms, advanced search capabilities, and applications that connect
to 3-D worlds (for example, Google Earth).

Having a solid awareness of the organization's Operational Intelligence and what tools can be used to obtain Operational Intelligence
gives Specialists an advantageous position from which they can continuously transform their business. This intelligence helps them make the
organization thrive in the face of adversity and ambiguity since it helps

to create a community of collective intelligence for learning new ways of thinking, behaving, performing, and becoming more agile.

One client we work with is using the Internet-based virtual world of Second Life to run team-building and information sessions for their organization. This helps the client to understand the workforce's demographics and its capabilities. It helps to keep people connected and allows them to more easily share information, all of which are keys for building Operational Intelligence. Wells Fargo is using Second Life to teach students in high school how to manage their finances, with the hope that these young minds will graduate and consider banking with Wells Fargo. This will help Wells Fargo to gain a better understanding on what potential customers will consider important in respect to products and services.

The Operational Intelligence Question

These examples support the competencies of the ABL Specialist and our thinking about Operational Intelligence. A leader with Operational Intelligence can easily answer the question, "What form of Operational Intelligence will we use to deliver information to individuals so they can make quick, accurate, and well-informed decisions?"

SPECIALIST TRAIT

#3

SPECIFIC EXPERTISE

Never become so much of an expert that you stop gaining expertise. View life as a continuous learning experience.

DENIS WAITLEY
Author and productivity consultant

Specific Expertise means having an in-depth understanding of the skills and knowledge required in a particular industry or sector. In our experience, we find Specific Expertise has been the traditional platform for organizations to maintain their unique competitive advantage. Our experience is that the leader who succeeds these days is the one who has the Specific Expertise to effectively and quickly understand the issues and ask facilitative questions about the process or topic area that will enable creative and efficient solutions. When this Specialist competency is combined with the other ABL roles and competencies, a higher level of competitive advantage can be achieved.

The Value of Specific Expertise

There has been an interesting shift in the value and importance of having Specific Expertise and its role in producing high-quality relevance and timeliness. At Carnegie Mellon University, Robert Kelley analyzed how much information the average knowledge worker should retain when doing his or her job. Since 1986, he has been asking people the question, "What percentage of the knowledge you need to do your job is stored in your own mind?" Kelley's results speak to the shift in thinking about obtaining and holding knowledge. The results might surprise you. In 1987, respondents answered that they needed to hold 75 percent of the knowledge in their heads. Ten years later, in 1997 the number dropped to 15 to 20 percent and nine years later, in 2006, the number dropped to 8 to 10 percent. That's a 65 percent drop in nineteen years. This study illustrates a dramatic trend toward people becoming just-in-time, "just-enough" information seekers in order to do their jobs, be experts, and survive in the current world where massive amounts of information are available almost instantly.

Kelley's research suggests that leaders who want to use and develop Specific Expertise need to take advantage of knowledge tools available to them rather than holding volumes of knowledge in their minds. The ABL Specialist recognizes the need for rapid knowledge transfer. He also knows that by sharing expertise, an organization can reduce duplication and competition for resources, and increase coordination and efficiency. ABLs know how and when to apply Specific Expertise at crucial times through planning and performance monitoring.

Knowledge Comes in Different Varieties

The key is that Specific Expertise is the combination of knowledge and skill sets. It does not require someone to be a brain surgeon or to have an enormously high level of intelligence. For example, Gillian Sorensen, a woman who was appointed by Secretary-General Kofi Annan to the United Nations Foundation, tells about a person being able to use the information she has to become an expert in negotiations. The United Nations Foundation is responsible for outreach to nongovernmental organizations and groups committed to peace, justice, development, and human rights. At the 3rd International Women's Peace Conference in Dallas, Texas, we were part of the facilitation group that helped create dialogue and lead strategic planning sessions for building the future of peace. During the conference Gillian told a story about the power of having and using grassroots knowledge and Specific Expertise. At a very basic level, having the ability to read, combined with a strong knowledge of technology, can have an enormous impact on a village.

Gillian told the story about a woman in Africa who was approached by a man who was traveling to her village to buy her goat. He offered the woman $4.00 for her goat. The woman had Specific Expertise in raising good goats and knew that her goats were of good quality. The man had the Specific Expertise in how to bargain and to get the lowest possible price for a goat. Sadly, in some Third World countries the illiteracy rate is very high. In some cases men and women sign work contracts with a fingerprint because they are illiterate. This woman made a point of learning how to read (something not common in this village), for she knew it would help her economically. She combined her ability to read with the ability to use technology and invested some of the money she raised from selling goats to purchase a cell phone. She knew communicating with other businesswomen would, in the end, help her business.

This African woman is part of a growing trend in the communication industry. It is an interesting point that Wireless Intelligence has exploded in developing countries. Twenty years ago, the first billion mobile phones were sold worldwide. The second billion sold in four years and the third billion sold in the last two years. The International Telecommunication Union says that 61 percent of mobile phones in the world are owned by people in developing countries (retrieved April 27, 2008, from http://www.itu.int/itunews/manager/display.asp?lang=en& year=2007&issue=07&ipage=Telecom-trends&ext=html 4-26-2008). Becoming literate and owning a cell phone has become part of an increase in economic status. Clearly, this woman in Africa was staying current with today's technology trends.

When the man made the offer of $4.00 for the goat, the African woman knew the market had been changing and she got on her cell phone to text message a friend in the next village to find out how much goats were selling for. She could do this only because she could read. The woman learned that in the next village goats were selling for $12.00. At that point she turned to the man and said she would sell the goat to him for $11.00. Because of her ability to read, her use of networking, and her agile business sense, she was able to negotiate a fair price.

What Specific Expertise Is Needed?

It goes without saying that the requirements for Specific Expertise in one person may be different from those in another. Expertise varies by location and circumstance. The key to this competence is that professional or academic qualifications are *not* mandatory for a person to be considered a specific expert. You might be an expert in accounting procedures, design work, embedded real-time software, or selling goats. Your expertise might be associated with a task or ability. Whatever your expertise, the criteria might change over time as the job requirements change along with the need to develop new capabilities.

To have Specific Expertise you must have

1. A high degree of proficiency, skill, and knowledge in a particular subject area or ability.
2. Analytical ability to assess a given situation as well as determine and organize key concepts.
3. Flexibility to retrieve important aspects of knowledge and approach new situations.

4. Agility in how to explore new strategies for self-improvement and self-awareness.
5. Ability to apply expertise at crucial times with forethought and strategic planning.
6. Recognition as a reliable resource who responds to context.
7. Cutting-edge knowledge to take the organization into the future.

The Specialist is the person who can convert Specific Expertise into performance, innovation, strategic thinking, and cross-pollination to achieve greater results.

The Specific Expertise Question

This list supports the competencies of ABL Specialists and their Specific Expertise. Leaders with these abilities can easily answer the question, "What level of proficiency, skills, and in-depth knowledge in a particular subject do I need to make quick, accurate, and well-informed decisions and exceed expectations?"

SPECIALIST TRAIT

#4

CORPORATE ACCOUNTABILITY

The path of least resistance is what
makes rivers and humans crooked.

ANONYMOUS

As we spend time working with corporations in North America, Asia Pacific, and Europe, we constantly find customers, stakeholders, and investors valuing corporate sustainability, social responsibility, and accountability. We began to wonder: if accountability is being considered as the elixir for finding solutions for everything from the national debt, increased performance, and changes in climate, then what do our clients think the word means? What we found was the concept of accountability has become a catch-all term referring to everything from cost control to professional ethics.

What Is Accountability?

In our search for a definition of accountability, we found twenty-four different ones. It is no wonder we sometimes experience different answers from our clients on what accountability means. For us, accountability is not simply about obeying laws, regulations, bureaucratic procedures, or hierarchical reporting relationships. Rather, accountability is about potentiality. It is about whether or not a person can give account—account-ability. To be accountable means you are required to answer for your actions. It means the person or organization must be answerable to someone or something outside themselves.

The word "answerability" is a synonym for "accountability," since accountability is the extent to which a person must answer to a higher authority (legal or organizational) for his or her actions. Using accountability and answerability interchangeably means a leader is accountable when he or she has made an obligation or has a willingness to accept responsibility for the consequences of his or her behavior. Leaders are accountable "for what" and "to whom." In our work with businesses we find that these accountable behaviors and actions are judged by standards of competency, integrity, judgment, prudence, vision, and/or courage.

Who Can Be Held Accountable?

According to authors Larry Cummings and Ron Anton in their report, the *Logical and Appreciative Dimensions of Accountability*, there are three fundamental criteria that must exist for a person to be held accountable.

To be held accountable, a person must have the capacity for

Rational behavior: The mental or psychological state of the person is that of a "normal adult." (You cannot have to account for your behavior if you are not capable of doing so.)

Ability to foresee events: Those results that any reasonable person could have anticipated in light of the information he or she was given.

Convergence: Not deviating from the expectations and actions for which you were held accountable.

What Can You Be Held Accountable For?

Robert Behn, of the Brookings Institution Press, believes you can hold someone accountable in one of three areas:

1. Accountability for Finances: This aspect is related to individual or departmental responsibility to perform a certain function. In this case accountability may be dictated or implied by law, regulation, or agreement.
2. Accountability for Fairness: This aspect deals with deciding what values should be upheld and creating rules, procedures, and standards to establish what the organization should and should not do. Records are kept, audits are conducted, and people are held accountable. If people do not do what they were required to do, they are punished.
3. Accountability for Performance: This aspect is related to purpose and providing the appropriate and required services to the "customer." It is about consequences and is related to achieving performance standards and satisfying performance expectations.

Holding people accountable is designed not solely to catch, reverse, and punish wrongdoing, but rather it is designed to deter wrongdoing. Accountability provides people with a mechanism to hold others responsible for abiding by certain laws, rules, and regulations that contribute to self-regulation. Since organizations are essentially dynamic systems (growing, developing, changing, and restructuring) without accountability as a distinct binding quality, leaders will find organizational life unstable and tenuous because of the absence of obligations and commitment.

The complexities and dynamics of promoting accountability require a leader to build relationships and provide people with opportunities to demonstrate their accomplishments and be held in account. To achieve Corporate Accountability as an outcome, the process requires the realization that a person's character and conduct will have an enormous impact on business results.

Accountability is not only an important business issue, but it is also a characteristic of great leaders. Historically great leaders have not only brought about momentous events by what they do, they have succeeded because of what they are. This would beg the question, what makes an accountable leader? We believe that greatness of a leader is obtained by the virtue of possessing certain personal qualities. One of those qualities is accountability.

In Eileen's research on accountability leading to a doctoral dissertation, she conducted interviews with fifteen individuals, including a three-star general, a chief financial officer, a lawyer, a three-time incarcerated drug addict, a superintendent of schools, a Boy Scout, a president of the American Indian Accountability Coalition, a pedophile profiler, an artist, a U.S. state auditor general, a disabled person, an international sales and marketing executive, and a county sheriff. She also surveyed 337 people from around the world, and conducted an extensive literature review looking for what personality traits contribute to accountable behavior. She wanted to determine what makes people accountable since there is a constant demand for accountability within organizations. In the end, she discovered a list of fourteen predominant personality traits that contribute to accountable behavior.

Traits of an Accountable Person

This list of traits describing an accountable person falls into two categories: self-management and commitment. This means an accountable person must have self-management skills to be called to account and must have a commitment to the cause as well as care enough to invest in the outcome.

1. Self-Management: Taking responsibility and action for personal performance; the person is reliable, can adjust to changing situations, and has a high standard of excellence.

2. Commitment: Making the obligation or pledge to carry out some action or to support some policy or person; the person has the inner strength to pursue the objective or task and remain focused to work hard without giving up on consistently giving attention to quality work.

The fourteen traits are:

1. Adaptability to others' demands *(Commitment)*
Is concerned with "being good." It indicates interest in being responsible and productive.

2. Agreeableness *(Commitment)*
Tends to be softhearted, good-natured, trusting, helpful, forgiving, and altruistic. Eager to help others, she or he tends to be responsive and empathic.

3. Awareness of expectations by others *(Commitment)*
Has an attention to meeting the *exact* expectations or requirements of others.

4. Being exact and correct *(Self-Management)*
Is alert to any failure in performance, procedures, change, and risks. He or she is interested in being competent at tasks and protecting against errors.

5. Caring and investing *(Commitment)*
Has a strong sense of the past and has a focus on the long-term perspective. She or he knows what has been done and how it has been done.

6. Collaboration *(Commitment)*
Is focused on mutual and reciprocal commitment to goals and objectives. He or she values teamwork, consensus, and inclusiveness, and is invested in others.

7. Crisp and clear thinking *(Self-Management)*
Is concerned that ideas be correct and clearly thought out.

8. Elitism or firm identity *(Self-Management)*
Has a clear sense of role and identity. Is comfortable with her or his self-image and shows congruence in her or his behaviors.

9. **Firm about standards** *(Self-Management)*
   Has an interest in evaluating a problem from the point of view of strongly held values and a sense of the limits in acceptable behavior. He or she has the ability to set limits and say NO to people and situations.
10. **Having a sense of community** *(Commitment)*
    Is concerned and aware of how others would like things done. She or he attends to group values and expectations.
11. **Interest in being strict** *(Self-Management)*
    Has a willingness to hold to standards in the face of opposition.
12. **Respectful response** *(Commitment)*
    Is responsible and wants to satisfy obligations.
13. **Service and support** *(Commitment)*
    Has the desire to interact with customers and others to provide support. He or she enjoys helping others meet their particular needs.
14. **Value-based** *(Self-Management)*
    Will attempt to view a problem objectively and develop solutions that are logical and rigorous.

Eileen's research confirmed that personality traits influence accountable behavior and, ultimately, accountability outcomes. Her research impacts the understanding about accountable leaders and what they need to bring to business to support corporate governance.

The Accountable Leader

Without a doubt, Agile Business Leaders have the traits of an accountable person. They are successful because of a perceived assured reliance of character, ability in talent, and the projection of truth. They perform functions for the benefit of another person or group and are focused more on meeting others' needs and less on their own.

Specialists maintain high moral and ethical standards and insist on accountability for themselves and the organization. If Corporate Accountability is good business, then having accountable leaders is the basic standard of corporate behavior necessary to sustain business. It is a circle of accountability, governance, and sustainability.

The Corporate Accountability Question

A leader having the competency of Corporate Accountability can easily answer the question, "What guidelines for processes, customs, policies, and laws are needed so people can do what is right for the organization and the community and deliver results with integrity?"

CONCLUSION TO SPECIALIST

During a coaching session with one of our clients we learned that he was a Freemason. (The Freemasons are one of the oldest and largest worldwide fraternities dedicated to moral uprightness and the development and maintenance of fraternal friendships.)

During our conversation, we were having an in-depth conversation about leadership. As the conversation moved toward the role of leader as a Specialist, he told us that Masonic students learn a primary lesson passed down to them from the ancient teachers. The ancient teachers say (and a lesson important for all Freemasons to learn), "Wisdom is the principal thing; therefore get wisdom: and with all thy getting, get understanding" (It should be noted that this phrase also appears in the Bible in Proverbs 4:7.)

What we have found in our work is that the only competitive advantage in an organization is the ability to learn, create ideas, and move those ideas into the marketplace in a profitable and expeditious way. This means organizations must rely more on the effectiveness in gathering, absorbing, and using the knowledge of its people as they create new concepts and solutions.

Corporate governance has its roots in the individuals who lead. A story about corporate governance and personal choice comes from one of our clients. One day a client's four-year-old daughter was very nasty to her sister. When our client caught her child she sat her down and said, "Mary, why did you take your sister's doll and cut off all of its hair? You know it's not your doll. You know how much your sister loves this doll. Didn't you hear a little voice inside you saying, 'Mary, this is not a good thing'?" Mary looked at her mother and said with great innocence and honesty, "Oh yeah, I heard that voice, but then I heard the other voice that said 'do it, do it' so I listened to that voice instead!" Again we emphasize that the strength of corporate governance originates from the people who lead and what "voices" inside themselves they choose to listen to.

The role of the Specialist is not only to gain knowledge, expertise, and wisdom. It is also to use the collective intelligence of those around her or him to build an understanding of how to be as effective as possible. The Specialist is required to have data-mining capabilities and an understanding of processes, technology, trends, and people. Specialists develop an organization that is adaptable and responsive to changing conditions. They offer a bold richness to the business capital of an organization. Today, leaders are working across geographic boundaries and in an integrated manner. They collaborate daily, regardless of distance or time-zone differences. It is these and other forces that keep Specialists needing to think, what does our workforce look like in terms of capabilities? What are the best sources for building talent? How can I develop myself to fill the roles that are needed in the emerging markets? ABL Specialists help to form networks, connecting people within the company as well as connecting with people from other industries or client bases.

The new reality for organizations is that leaders and employees are engines of success. They must respond nimbly to customers, function in more complex ways, take initiative, be adaptable, and work in collaboration with all stakeholders.

Ideas in Action

The Cartaphor on page 182 was developed in 2009 as part of a creative thinking tool and communication mechanism to develop the vision for a prominent Shanghai-based project management company called Firsttrack. Firsttrack's claim to fame is its work on the Shanghai Maglev, a fast train that runs from the Pudong airport into Shanghai at speeds of 430 km/hr. We first started working with Firsttrack in 2008 to help them achieve the next step in their development to become an agile organization.

Transforming an organization in this part of the world requires some culturally relevant and respectful techniques to get the undiscussibles to discussibility. The leadership team at Firsttrack developed this Cartaphor in a series of workshops and work groups over a period of three months. Our facilitation included an added challenge because it involved us guiding the process in English with real-time translation in Mandarin. The group had an extra surprise during the process when they discovered that one of their leaders, the concrete supervisor, was an artist, and he volunteered to draw the entire Cartaphor for the company. This discovery made the process even more personal for the group.

The leaders' discussions about vision, values, and mission provided clarity of their "desired future state" and what was needed to get there. This process helped the leadership team become aligned in its quest to become a more successful, internationally connected business.

In 2010 Firsttrack reported a 100 percent increase in profit and a significant increase in its program of future work (quite a business case for becoming agile). Clearly the company knows how to align its Specialists to produce results in the organization.

QUESTIONS TO CONSIDER

The following questions are designed to increase your creativity and challenge some of your current thinking. They are designed to help you develop a more agile mindset. Imagine yourself using this Cartaphor in your role as a Specialist to answer the following questions.

1. Think about the brilliant future on the hill in the distance. What additional industry knowledge do you need to get to the top of the hill?
2. What messages are being transmitted from the satellite to the people below?
3. What is the man saying to the lineup of new recruits in the bottom right section of the Cartaphor?

4. If the people arriving in the boats are auditors coming to assess the town, what are they going to find? What do the people in the town need to prepare for the auditors' visit?

5. Where are you located in this Cartaphor? What are you doing as a leader to help reach the vision for the organization?

6. Is any component or service missing in this picture that should be included for the organization's future success?

7. How does this Cartaphor relate to the emerging changes your organization is experiencing in the industry?

PERSONAL ACTION PLAN

Self-assessment and adaptability are extremely important as an Agile Business Leader. We suggest you devise a personal plan to accomplish changes you want to implement for yourself or your organization. Ask the question, "What actions or changes in my behavior do I need to accomplish and by when?" Then construct an Action Plan that will help you achieve your goal. Write it down and monitor it or use your community of practice to help you become even more accountable for your actions.

Action Plan

	Action Item	Resources Required	Date of Completion
1			
2			
3			
4			

What actions or changes in my behavior do I need to accomplish? How soon?

_____

_____

_____

6

CONCLUSION

Throughout the years the views of what constitutes a leader have changed considerably. Some people think leaders are physically strong and abnormally hard workers. Some think leaders are born, not made, making leadership a condition of destiny. Others believe that with the right teaching and breeding, any person can become an excellent leader. In the "new economy," where technology is predominant and the pace of business seems to be accelerating exponentially, the need to respond quickly and be innovative and resilient has become a necessity. This more appropriate style of leadership requires a balanced approach between the business capital and the human capital of the organization. This Agile Business Leader approach to leadership has become a necessity in the world we operate within.

If you ask a firefighter he or she will tell you, in the case of fire, the first task is to extinguish the flames, then seek the cause. That advice holds true for leadership across the globe. Today leaders must have the capacity to respond quickly, share information, and access vast amounts of technological, product, and financial information. They must be able to respond to a myriad of people issues while at the same time coping with immediate issues.

For those who believe the "one size fits all" leadership mentality is the way to go, let us be the bearers of bad news: that way of thinking has come to an end. We suggest considering some counsel from the new generation of workers and, by deduction, the next generation of leaders.

Those working in organizations will be willing to contribute if they feel the company values their skills and talents. This a time for leaders to demonstrate a way forward and face immense and ambiguous problems head-on and lead people toward success. In an era filled with confusion, contradictions, and corruption, the world is calling for Agile Business Leaders.

What makes the ABL model pragmatic is the reality that there is no one best way to lead. There is no particular leadership style found that proves universally satisfactory in every situation. What we do know is that successful leaders tend to have agility in dealing with different situations in an appropriate and effective manner. They use their agility to create a clear sense of direction and a flexible repertoire of behaviors. It is the leader who can listen, delegate, involve, decide, adapt, respond, and direct who will be the most successful over time.

Agile Business Leaders take risks and accept losses. They are committed, are consistent, and continually learn and challenge themselves and others. These are the leaders who are willing to shake up assumptions about existing routines and processes. They motivate people and create the momentum, which gets people excited about achievements and things they may have never seen before, something that does not yet exist. ABLs know that knowledge must flow rapidly and freely from expert sources directly to the people who need it.

The world is screaming for flexible and responsive leaders who can innovate rapidly and wisely and who can reduce time to market on goods and services. It is the ABL who can thrive in this new, fast-paced environment and lead within the midst of fierce and chaotic competition.

There an enormous difference between leading an organization and presiding over it. The leader who boasts of a "hands-off" approach and puts faith in empowerment is not dealing with the issues at hand. The Agile Business Leader confronts people responsible for poor performance or gets into the trenches to help search for problems and create solutions. It is the ABL's high-octane capacity for being nimble and collaborative with the skills to adapt quickly to new, different, or changing requirements that creates successful results.

Agile Business Leaders are known for their capacity to

1. Understand themselves and the impact they have on others.
2. Enable action through collaborative deployment techniques.
3. Optimize their options by thinking strategically.
4. Continuously create business intelligence.
5. Create balance by planning for expected change and preparing for unexpected change.
6. Anticipate when the rules of business will change.
7. Understand priorities by having a comprehensive understanding of the business and industry.
8. Adapt and quickly respond to rapidly changing conditions.

Organizations have reason to ponder their mortality these days. They now compete in faster, more complex, and more volatile markets. This has caused a "new normal" to emerge. As the concepts of organizational leadership advance, theorists, "pracademics," gurus, and practitioners will begin to focus on the fundamental capacity of organizations to adapt to rapidly changing conditions and to do so over and over again. The key to sustaining competitiveness is learning agility and how to become an Agile Business Leader.

More than two hundred years ago, in 1775, Thomas Paine, a British writer and publicist, wrote, "We have it in our power to begin the world all over again. A situation similar to the present hath not appeared since the days of Noah until now. The birthday of a new world is at hand" (*Common Sense, and the Turning Point to American Independence* pamphlet, lines 21–22). In these times of ambiguous challenges, leaders need to find extraordinary reserves of energy and enthusiasm. The dominant patterns of leadership within an organization must serve their workforces on multiple levels—meeting multiple needs and offering multiple strategies for cultural, structural, process, and technology-support elements. During the roller coaster of exhilarating highs and depressing lows as the future evolves, learning how to learn and having the capacity for collaborative and interactive working behaviors are what will lead to an organization's success.

Leaders need to recognize "a new world is at hand" and demand that a new breed of leader does not merely add on elements of a new philosophy or principles of leadership to what they are already doing. Instead, these new leaders become highly adaptive leaders who can execute strategies and produce results in unstable environments. This new type of leader has the ability to create adaptable resources and drive results throughout the organization. They are the leaders who can sail through turbulent, brackish waters with a clear horizon in mind.

The Agile Business Leader model presented in this book is intended to rattle mental cages and expand individual consciousness. The model presents a holistic view of the roles, traits, and competencies we have experienced in successful global leaders who are excelling in taking their organizations into the future.

> The ABL roles are shorthand labels to describe the four key areas a leader must be proficient in. An Agile Business Leader is proficient in *all four ABL roles.*
>
> The ABL traits are the permanent patterns of behavior of the leader, even when that leader is faced with different and difficult situations during difficult and different times.
>
> The ABL competencies are the skills, abilities, talents, and knowledge a leader possesses to be adaptable, responsive and resilient.

The ABL approach is a holistic one, based on the philosophy that business success on the global stage can be achieved only by building leadership abilities in every person within the organization and not just in a small select group. By drawing out and leveraging people's strengths, an organization can maximize individual performance and potential. Agile Business Leaders withstand the test of time because they are authentic and courageous and value capability. They never forget the power of engaging human capability. This is a lesson General Peter Schoomaker, as commander in chief of the U.S. Special Operations Command, learned in 1980. As a leader, "General Schoomaker was one of the youngest officers to take part in Desert One, the failed attempt to rescue Americans held hostage in Iran. Today Schoomaker keeps a photo on his desk of one of the downed helicopters from that mission—a reminder to himself of a core principle: Never confuse enthusiasm with capability" (retrieved March 15, 2010, from http://www.fastcompany .com/magazine/27/operation.html).

We know from our work that human talent and capability are abundant resources. They are also the ultimate generators of the intangibles that drive the creation of success in the digital age. As a leader, whether you are operating a paper mill, a pharmaceutical company, a restaurant, or an architectural firm, the ABL model is designed for the new future of leadership—a future of fast-changing technologies, unpredictable market pressures, economic breakthroughs, and the need to reduce cost.

Agile Business Leaders are the central ingredient for developing an organization and helping it survive and thrive. Even Charles Darwin knew that the ability to be agile and adaptive to one's environment (even more than strength) was the quality required and key to survival.

We hope this book has helped you define yourself as a leader and armed you with the capability to design agility into the way you lead.

INDEX

learning *(continued)*
  developing a sustainable environment for, 113–14
  as a team, 45
Learning in Action, as an element of an Enabler's traits, 90, 94, 108–14
Leighton Asia, 11
Lencioni, Patrick, 122–23
lifecycle development, 61
Lim, Vivien, 104
linear economy, 60–61
linking, organizational goals to individuals' motivation, 64
Logical and Appreciative Dimensions of Accountability (Cummings and Anton), 174–75
loop economy, 60
Lordstown Syndrome, 117

M

MAKE (Most Admired Knowledge Enterprises) program, 167
many-sidedness, theory of, 125
Maslow, Abraham, 25
mastery, personal, 44–45
maturity, value of, 102
McDonough, William, 61
mental abilities, strengthening, 148
mental models, 44, 45
metacognition, 163–64
Middle East, strategic development in, 85–86
mobile phones, expanding use of, 171–72
morale, 128–29
Motivation
  causes of, 106
  as an element of an Enabler's traits, 90, 94, 104–8
  influences on, 107
  theories of, 105

undesirable results of, 106–7
Mountaineering in Scotland (Murray), 149–50
multitasking, for Agile Business Leaders, 12
Murray, W. N., 149–50

N

National Broadcasting Company (NBC), 78
New Knowledge Organisation, The (Sigismund), 162
Newman, Paul, 23
normative commitment, 151
Novozymes, 11

O

onboarding, 105, 110, 120
openness, as a Resource for Innovation, 74
Operational Intelligence
  tools for, 168
  as trait of Specialists, 168–69
opportunities, 22–23
optimism, 149
organizational change process, two generations of, 10
organizational commitment, 149, 151–52
organizational culture, 114–15
organizational plans, 76
organizational success, abilities needed for, 96–97
organizations
  influences on, 49–54
  performance of, linked to attitudes of its people, 54
  as systems, 44–49
Outcomes, as elements of an Enabler's traits, 90, 94–104

ABOUT THE AUTHORS

EILEEN DOWSE, Ph.D., is a recognized organizational psychologist specializing in organizational health and effectiveness through training, consulting, cultural assessments, and performance management. She works with individuals, teams, and large-scale systems to facilitate strategic change throughout North America, Europe, and Asia. She fosters productive relationships for organizations and strengthens employee commitment to ensure greater levels of teamwork. She is among the international leaders in facilitation. She is co-founder and chair for the International Institute for Facilitation and a certified master facilitator. Eileen uses common sense wisdom and innovative ideas to offer exceptional professionalism and customized services.

BARRY BREWSTER is a principal with Evans and Peck, a member of the WorleyParson Group, specializing in facilitating change in a variety of business environments. With more than twenty-five years of experience in Asia Pacific, Europe, and North America, he works on optimizing business performance through positive change in strategy, systems, processes, and people. Clients seek out Barry because he successfully helps them leverage the knowledge and wisdom within their organization to produce sustainable results. Barry is a board member of the International Institute for Facilitation and a certified master facilitator. Barry's unique ability to facilitate learning, energize people toward innovation, and bring about change is what makes him an AGILE leader in the industry.

www.ingramcontent.com/pod-product-compliance
Lightning Source LLC
Chambersburg PA
CBHW070542200326
41519CB00013B/3102